PUBLISHER

TOM MASCHLER

PUBLISHER

PICADOR

First published 2005 by Picador
an imprint of Pan Macmillan Ltd
Pan Macmillan, 20 New Wharf Road, London N1 9RR
Basingstoke and Oxford
Associated companies throughout the world
www.panmacmillan.com

ISBN 0 330 48420 6

1 3 5 7 9 8 6 4 2

A CIP catalogue record for this book is available from
the British Library.

Typeset by SetSystems Ltd, Saffron Walden, Essex
Printed and bound in Great Britain by
Mackays of Chatham plc, Chatham, Kent

For Regina, who put up with me throughout the writing and wherever we found ourselves. Even when camping in Namibia. For my children Hannah, Alice and Ben, who never ceased to ask after my progress and encouraged me at all times. And for the memory of my father and of my mother, Rita.

CONTENTS

Preface

For me the most important aspect of publishing is the relationship with authors and the editing of their books. Of the many writers and artists I have worked with a few have especially excited me: Joseph Heller, whose *Catch-22* was the very first novel I bought at Cape and which became a spectacular success; John Fowles, who came into my life shortly thereafter with *The Collector*, followed by *The Magus* and *The French Lieutenant's Woman*; Salman Rushdie, whose *Midnight's Children* was a memorable novel and remains my favourite of all his books; Doris Lessing and Kurt Vonnegut, both of whom have become lifelong friends; the man I consider to be the greatest living novelist, the Colombian writer Gabriel García Márquez, whose work I first encountered in Cuba forty years ago; Roald Dahl, the supreme writer for children; Lucian Freud, the greatest living English painter; Desmond Morris, the zoologist, world-renowned for *The Naked Ape*; John Lennon, whose verse, prose and drawings in his books *In His Own Right* and *A Spaniard in the Works* are in a category of their own; Quentin Blake, the wonderful illustrator for children; Henri Cartier-Bresson, the celebrated photographer.

And then of course there was Ernest Hemingway. Luck often plays a role in publishing and it was especially applicable to the way I found myself editing this most famous Cape author.

PROLOGUE: *A Moveable Feast*

I WAS TWENTY-SEVEN when Hemingway killed himself, and I had just joined Cape. Being a part of Hemingway's publishing house gave me a particular sense of pride. I met him only once and that was prior to my becoming a publisher. It was an encounter at a bullfight in Malaga. He was with Kenneth Tynan, who played the great aficionado and introduced me to Hemingway somewhat reluctantly. None the less the meeting, though only very brief, gave me some small sense of the man.

A month or so after Hemingway's death Bob Wren Howard (co-founder of Jonathan Cape) introduced me to Mary, Hemingway's widow, while she was visiting our publishing house. I recall feeling that we got on rather well, which is to say that she seemed to like me. And then a few days later Wren Howard asked me into his office. He announced, clearly with some pride, that Mary had taken a shine to me and I was invited out to Idaho, Hemingway's principal place of residence. Mary wanted me to help her assemble the manuscript on which 'Papa' had been working when he shot himself. The task was to make a book out of various articles and notes dealing mainly with Hemingway's youth in France and with his friends at the time. They included Ford Madox Ford, James Joyce and Scott Fitzgerald, although of course none of these giants was famous then. You may imagine my excitement at this assignment. The fact that it had come up so early in my life at Cape made it all the more special.

A week later I found myself on the way to Ketchum, Idaho, Hemingway's local town. Mary was at the tiny airport to meet me, wearing a much-used Stetson and the statutory kerchief. She drove a beat-up old green convertible Cadillac. We passed through Ketchum, a small place straight out of a Western, and then took off for the ranch which was not far away. In the car I looked at Mary as though for the first time. Her face was deeply bronzed and much lined, with great energy. Her hair was cut short, with streaks of blonde. She had clearly been pretty. However, there was a toughness to her which I suspected had always been there.

The ranch was in a dip surrounded by wooded hills on all sides, a beautiful location but lacking in sunshine. The house itself was constructed like a massive log cabin. This is where I was to spend six days. I cannot say that I warmed to the environment but I was so much looking forward to fulfilling my mission that this was irrelevant.

Most of our time was spent immersed in the trunk which Hemingway had stacked with magazines and manuscript pages.

There was no indication of the shape he had envisaged for his book. This made our task simultaneously more difficult and more rewarding since we had to make our own choices. From the first morning we began reading and we placed the material in what we thought to be a chronological order. Frequently we came across several versions of the same event and had the satisfaction of selecting the one we thought best. We worked all day, every day, except the third day when we were invited to go out shooting.

Mary surprised me by suggesting I use Papa's safari gun. It was a monster of a gun and made me extremely nervous. When I discovered that our quarry was doves I became less concerned. The chances of my hitting even a single one of these tiny birds was exceedingly remote. None the less I did take a shot or two. I was inspired by the memory of having been a reasonably good shot while in the Air Force. But this gun was extremely heavy. Although it seemed an absurd pursuit to me, I greatly enjoyed our 'day off'. It was followed by an exciting discovery. The next day I came across a reference Papa had made, in his own hand, to 'a moveable feast'. I thought it would make a wonderful title and Mary felt the same way. We were encouraged by the fact that we now had a title we could be proud of, and our task became to create a book worthy of it. The material was magnificent. Hemingway would describe a girl sitting in a café in 1922 and the reader is transported to that moment and to seeing the girl in the café in Paris at the time. There were many wonderful scenes but it was not easy to make them flow into a continuous whole. The magic of Hemingway's prose is frequently spoken of and *A Moveable Feast* is filled with examples.

I remember that every night we ate somewhat indifferent steaks. We were always alone but I have little recollection of our conversation. I know only that I did my best to entertain Mary and that it was not easy. Very understandably she seemed depressed. Then one night we were invited to the home of Hemingway's doctor. Together with several of Hemingway's companions, he had just returned from Canada, where they had been shooting mountain goat. The flavour of the meat served that evening resembled venison. It had a more subtle flavour than any game I had ever eaten.

This had been their first hunting trip without Hemingway. The doctor, who led the party, was a great burly man. Over the years he had become a close friend of Hemingway and they had frequently gone shooting together. Far from being spent mourning the great man's death, the evening was a cheerful event. Inevitably, the conversation centred around Hemingway anecdotes. At the doctor's house Mary, along with everyone else, enjoyed drinking wine with dinner. At home she drank nothing but whisky. She would begin a couple of hours before dinner, continue right through the meal, and then on into the night. She must have consumed at least a bottle every evening and, not surprisingly, she invariably got drunk. I can't be sure, but I think she would have liked me to have gone to bed with her, although I sensed that this was more out of desperation than desire. When I had met her in London she seemed unhappy but now she was deeply sad and lonely. Clearly the gap left by Hemingway's death was the more painful in her own home.

On my penultimate night Mary suddenly pointed to the porch which led into the house from the main door. This was where Papa's safari gun stood, the one I had used on our little hunt. 'That is where Papa shot himself,' Mary said. Naturally this gave me a frisson and I realized that all along I'd had an intuition that something sinister had occurred on that porch. Since my arrival we had never entered the house by this front entrance. Mary had gone out of her way to avoid it.

We managed to complete our work on the very last night before my departure. That evening Mary wrapped up the book and asked me to deliver the package to Scribner, Hemingway's New York publisher of long standing. She wanted me to hand it over personally to a man called Harry Brague, who had become Hemingway's editor after the death of the celebrated Maxwell Perkins. I knew Brague a little but had no idea whether he was aware of my editorial role in this venture. However, I was certain that if he knew of it he would have been deeply disapproving. He was a proud man and it would have been difficult for him not to feel slighted. I promised Mary I would take the book directly to him and it was my intention to do so. But when I walked down Fifth Avenue and reached the Scribner office I felt too embarrassed to go through with it. And so I wrote Harry Brague's name on the parcel and dropped it off with the receptionist.

This occurred forty years ago. Since then I have re-read *A Moveable Feast* many times. Perhaps my intimacy with the book makes me biased but it seems to me a small masterpiece. It is certainly the most evocative book imaginable. Hemingway believed that to write well all you had to do was to write truthfully. *A Moveable Feast* is a perfect example of just this. Although it deals with only a few years of Hemingway's life, the book represents the experiences of a lifetime.

PART ONE

EARLY DAYS

I WAS BORN in Berlin in 1933. My father was a commercial traveller in the book business. He did not show up until three days after my birth. His trip must have been going well. In 1938 we moved from Berlin to Vienna. This turned out to be a serious misjudgement, for Hitler marched into Austria shortly afterwards. It was an unhappy period for me and I had my own way of expressing my discontent. To give one example, I made sure I was the first to wake up in our household and I would collect my father's post from the doormat and then hide it under my mattress. This continued for a period of several weeks. I even took the precaution of leaving the odd letter behind to avoid suspicion. Naturally my father was beside himself when my mattress was turned and the letters were discovered.

The very day after the Anschluss my dad arrived at his office in Vienna to be greeted by the entire staff of five with 'Heil Hitler' in conjunction with the Nazi salute. Shortly afterwards two officers came to our house to arrest my father. He had committed three crimes: he was Jewish, he was a socialist, and he was a publisher. Fortunately he was away on another trip. In his absence they confiscated the house together with all its contents, including my father's precious collection of first editions. He also owned manuscripts and letters by important writers, among them Thomas Mann and Hermann

Hesse, and with his particular passion for painters he even possessed a few letters by van Gogh and Cézanne. I remember that my mother, Rita, packed a small suitcase with articles of clothing and I had my little rucksack. It contained an item particularly close to my heart. The officer had invited me to take one object from my father's study. I chose a long, thick pencil, red at one end and blue at the other.

By a circuitous route we made our way to England and my father followed a few months later. My mother and I caught the last boat from Holland to Sweden but there we missed the final departure for New York, which was originally to have been our destination. Instead we arrived in England. But for this I would have become a young American boy and I suppose I might also have become a young American publisher. All four grandparents remained in Germany and we later discovered that three of them had been gassed in the camps.

At first we stayed in London with my uncle Alfons, my mother's brother, who was a doctor. The war got under way and children were evacuated whenever possible. My mother came across an advertisement for a 'lady cook' in a large country house near Henley-on-Thames. The job entailed working for the De Salis family. Lady De Salis was a tyrant. She suffered from acute arthritis and could be heard clattering along the tiles with her two sticks as she made her way to the kitchen each morning. She seemed to delight in tormenting my mother, who had never worked for anyone before. Our little hamlet was called Crazies Hill. We were accommodated in the coach-house.

I was six and attended the local village school, the Robert Piggott Junior School. My mother's employers referred to it as 'the street-kid school'. It will come as no great surprise to learn that I was not allowed to play with the grandchildren of the house. I avenged myself from time to time by stealing a precious nectarine from the greenhouse. More daringly, I also stole some wooden lifeboats that were resting along the deck of a massive galleon which stood proudly in the hallway of the main house. Initially there were two rows of lifeboats, one on each side of the masts. I stole a pair from one end. I then stole two more from the other end to even things up, so to speak. And then the same again; a further two from each end. By this time the lifeboat showing was so thin that, to be on the safe side, I also took the rest of the boats.

My school was a bleak stone building. We could not afford the bus and so I walked there every day. It took me almost an hour each way. I got to know the local people and would cheerfully greet them as I passed by. I also got to know many birds in the hedges, especially in the spring when they laid their eggs and hatched their babies. The birds made my walk a wonderful adventure. I never took a single egg although they were so beautiful and so tempting. I learned to recognize the chaffinch, the blackbird, the sparrow, the robin, the wren and many others. The walk sometimes seemed very long and boring but I was never afraid.

At school I was a novelty and the other children did not seem to know what to make of me. It was easy to form my own little gang. Although this was sixty years ago I still remember some of the children. There was Anne Stringer, a lanky girl, and Eric Webb, short, tough and a bit of a bully. And then there was Rosemary Rideout, a pretty girl I secretly fancied. Anne's parents owned the greengrocer's and Rosemary's father had the garage. Some twenty years ago I took my children on a pilgrimage to Wargrave. I found it enormously reassuring that the Rideout garage and Stringer's greengrocery were still in business. I thought of introducing myself but for fear of disappointment did not do so.

My gang's most exciting activity was 'scrumping'. This is a country word for stealing apples. The orchards were located at wealthy homes outside the village. We sold the booty to local people and the proceeds were shared equally among us. I well

remember returning home to Crazies Hill and handing my earnings over to my mother. My contribution was only small but I felt pride in being something of a bread-earner. Another means I employed for making money was to hang about a nearby US Army camp. I used the catchphrase: 'Got any gum, chum?' and I would be offered large packs of chewing-gum and tins of marmalade. The latter especially had a good resale value. At the camp (remember I was only nine) I would invite a soldier or two to come to tea with my mother at our coachman's cottage. Naturally I chose the best-looking. There was one called Fred, whom I thought my mother rather fancied. Certainly she went out to the cinema with him in nearby Henley. At the time my father was working in London as an air-raid warden on a volunteer basis. He would spend most weekends with us while he waited for the war to end and for some profitable employment.

At the end of the war, to my father's amazement, a trunk belonging to us turned up on a railway siding in Rotterdam. It had apparently sat there since 1939. Now this trunk contained my teddy bear: a bear I had frequently imagined in the intervening years as 'enormous'. The bear I recalled was at least two feet high. When the trunk finally arrived in London it contained an average nine-inch bear. It makes good sense that when I was parted from my teddy bear, aged five, he should have seemed a giant.

At the beginning life in England was relatively good and then, as the war progressed and most of the servants left, my mother's job deteriorated to waitress, butler, pantry-maid and then charlady as well as cook. After four years in the village school I got a grant to go to Leighton Park, a minor Quaker public school near Reading. Unfortunately the grant did not stretch to my being a full-time boarder and so for two years I was lodged with six different families. Although everyone was extremely kind to me, both the boys and their parents, I found moving to a new home three times a year a depressing experience. Being a displaced person seemed to be my fate.

SCHOOL AND TRAVEL

Before I went to Leighton Park there was an interlude in France. My mother had decided that I should learn French 'properly' and that meant learning the language in France. In order to achieve this successfully she wanted me to spend a summer with French people who spoke no English. Now that I was just twelve years old this seemed the right moment to her. Since she did not know an appropriate family she determined to find one. Her method was to take me to Brittany where she chose Roscoff, a fishing village on the north coast. No sooner had we arrived than she took off down the high street and began to knock upon the front doors of whichever houses she thought looked promising. Her proposition was simple. The family should offer me board and lodging for which they would be paid at cost and I should remain with them for the summer. There seemed to be precious little in it from the French family's point of view and that is no doubt the reason why a dozen households turned us down. I was growing increasingly embarrassed and then, at what looked like the grandest house of all, we struck lucky. It was a bonus that the house happened to belong to the Mayor of Roscoff. He had two sons and a very pretty daughter, all approximately my age.

During my stay I did not receive so much as a single phone call from my mother and just two letters. It was part of her method, no doubt. The second of the letters dealt entirely with arrangements for my return. Whilst she had regarded her presence as important on the outward journey, it seemed to her entirely superfluous for the way back. She reckoned there was no reason why at the age of twelve I should not find my own way to England. Of course she turned out to be right. She was also right to suppose that I would become reasonably fluent in French.

A week after my return, term began at Leighton Park. I did reasonably well scholastically. Perhaps more importantly from the school's point of view, I became tennis champion and also squash champion. But for me the most challenging competition at school was the speech competition. This fell into two categories: unprepared speeches, where you were given a subject, say 'Comics', immediately prior to being catapulted on to the stage in front of the entire school. Your task was to speak for three minutes. The other, and much more highly esteemed category, was the prepared speech competition. Here a shortlist of three contestants would be required to make a ten-minute speech in front of the upper school and parents. I managed to get into the final but failed to win. My parents usually came down to school for the speech competition. They intended to be supportive but I could not help dreading my mother's outrageous clothes, and my father's manner in cross-examining the teachers at tea-time always felt alienating to me.

There was one other competition which held a special appeal for me. It was known as the Travel Scholarship. Contestants were required to write an account of a journey they proposed to undertake. My entry was based upon an ambition to visit Israel, to tour the country, and especially to spend some time working in several kibbutzim.

I won the competition. However, in making the announcement, the headmaster qualified my win by declaring that it must be 'subject to practicability'. The award was for £100 and it was a condition that the winning entry be achievable for that expenditure. The condition filled me with a mixture of anger and determination. In my application I had stated that I would hitchhike to Marseille and then 'work my passage' (this normally entails washing dishes) on a boat to Haifa. I was sixteen, and the big question was exactly how I proposed to get such a job. I was confident that I could do so but was required to prove it. And so I wrote to Ben-Gurion, the Israeli Prime Minister. I explained my dilemma and asked if he could help.

I was convinced that he would. I really was. He wrote back to say he had passed my letter on to the Ministry of Transport and Communications. From then on it was plain sailing. The Ministry instructed me to report to the Marseille office of the Israeli Kedmah Line on a certain day at the end of June and to be ready to sail the following day.

Of all my memories of the trip it was the physical labour of working in a kibbutz that gave me the greatest satisfaction. And to this was added the pleasure of sharing the work with men and women from all walks of life. It was not unusual to find oneself shovelling dung alongside a professor of philosophy from Heidelberg University. This of course could only happen in such a new and idealistic country.

When I came back to school two months after returning from Israel, the headmaster summoned me to discuss my future. I said that I wanted to go to university. Oxford or Cambridge. He said that I did not have the brains to get into either. So I was determined. I worked like mad, and I was offered a place to read PPE at St Edmund Hall, Oxford. A few weeks later I decided that I would prefer to read English. The Principal of my future college suggested I visit him. When I got there he had all my papers spread out in front of him. He said, 'I see you were tennis champion. Hum, and squash champion as well.' I said, 'Excuse me, but is that relevant?' He said, 'Well, your marks were not very good. I feel you should stay with PPE.' I replied, 'Are you saying that you offered me a place because of the tennis and the squash?' I wrote to him not long thereafter, thanking him, but saying that I would not be coming up after all. It seems surprising to me that throughout my career I have never even once been asked whether I went to university. Everyone simply assumes that I did.

Instead I decided to use the three years I would have spent at university on some extensive travel and learning Spanish and Italian. But first of all I wanted to fulfil a dream. This was to hitchhike all the way around the United States. When I look back on my journey I don't know how it was achieved. I arrived with £5 (then $13) and travelled all the way around America. It was illegal to work without a permit but I did get the odd job regardless. The most dramatic of these was working on the island of San Pedro (off Los Angeles), scraping tuna fish in a canning factory. The fish was boiled in an enormous vat and we removed the skin with very long, sharp knives. The stench was horrendous. I was the only white man – almost all the others were Puerto Ricans. Another temporary job I took was road-building in Chicago. It was thirst-making work in the summer heat. But what made the experience memorable was that at the end of the second day the boss invited me to join him for some beers. He announced that he had never met an Englishman who could not hold his liquor. Of course I took this as a challenge and drank a dozen cans, equalling his dozen. On my way home I threw up and lay down on the pavement, my head up against a wall, to sleep it off.

Everyone found me a novelty on the road and the hospitality I received was astonishing. On the whole it was easy to get lifts, except on one occasion when I stood waiting for eight hours in a temperature of 110 degrees. I finally walked six miles to a petrol station and learned that the reason no one had stopped was that there had been a murder in the region.

It was in Texas that a truck driver turned to me and asked, 'What language do you all speak over in England?' I found it exceedingly difficult to persuade him that the English I spoke was my native tongue rather than an effort on my part to speak American.

On several occasions I was arrested for vagrancy. The sum varies from state to state but it was illegal not to be in possession of a minimum of $10–20. More than once the sheriff took me to his home for the night and invited me to have dinner with his family instead of putting me in gaol.

For me, the high points of my journey were Las Vegas, New Orleans and the Grand Canyon. To be able to experience these disparate and extraordinary places on virtually no money is a great privilege. But perhaps the most glorious of all my memories is the unique sense of freedom and excitement that hitchhiking offers in a country as large and as varied as America.

I returned to New York with slightly more money than when I set out but nothing like enough to pay for the cheapest fare back to England. So I wandered into the *New York Times* building. I knew no one who worked there. My only credential was the article that had appeared in the *Los Angeles Times* about my adventures, alongside a photograph of me. I showed it to the Editorial Department and persuaded one of the staff to commission me to write an article for them. The *New York Times* produced my piece handsomely, alongside a cartoon of me on the road. They also paid very well. The article appeared more than fifty years ago and I still possess a copy of it.

Back in England, I was eager to earn some money. The most lucrative job I found was with a travel company called Global. My task was to act as a tour guide to coach parties around Europe. I had thirty-six passengers at a time, mainly American. I received a good salary and tips as well. The more initiative I showed, the bigger the tips. I was quite inventive. We spent one night in Venice and I invariably organized a gondola trip. On the gondola ride itself I did not make a profit, but the musical aspect of the evening was a different matter. To hire a band to accompany a gondola costs a fortune. So much so that only a few very rich honeymoon couples could indulge in such a thing. I would tip my gondolier to follow a pair of lovers who had hired their 'private' music. My tourists would then sit in their gondolas, all in a row, trailing behind the music. I charged each passenger an additional £2 for the privilege, and of course the music cost me nothing. With a £10 (generous) tip to the gondolier, I made a profit of £62 a night. And everyone was happy, except of course the honeymoon couple.

Being a tour guide was extremely hard work but I earned a great deal of money. Enough to buy first one, then two, houses in Chalcot Crescent, at the foot of London's Primrose Hill.

Next came National Service. I chose the Russian Corps (a branch of the Air Force) because I thought I would learn something useful. I had not realized that the course would be preceded by three months of 'square bashing'. This had absolutely nothing to do with learning Russian. We were engaged in absurd pastimes such as digging a trench one day and filling it in the next. My mates had no problem with such pursuits but I found them intolerable. And then, on one occasion, we were inspected by a drunk officer. I was so outraged that I decided to go on a hunger strike. My strike lasted three weeks without even a crust of bread though I did drink water. The strike gave me a great sense of peace. I announced most calmly that I was not prepared to waste any more time with the Air Force. I remember the sergeant who came screaming at me in my hut while the others were eating lunch. I spoke quite softly and asked him kindly not to shout. He was at a loss and called in the head of the camp. This man announced that he would transfer me to a military hospital. Within half an hour an ambulance had arrived and I was taken to what was clearly a lunatic asylum. As I entered I made what I was later told is the classic remark: 'Why are you taking me here? I am not crazy.'

Whatever my state of mind, it was obvious that most of the inmates were genuinely mad. A good number of them seemed to think that they were Jesus Christ. I found life among mad people strangely attractive. One felt totally free. If an orderly handed you a plate of food that you didn't want it was fine simply to throw the plate back at him. Compared with that of the others, my behaviour was exemplary.

I must confess that I had one very important factor in my favour. This was that I had attended a Quaker school. The officers knew that most Quakers are conscientious objectors and of course conscientious objectors are exempt from joining a fighting force. So when I announced that despite my Quaker education I was not a conscientious objector, this was viewed as most honourable on my part. I suspect it may account for my being released from the hospital after a mere three weeks.

Not only was I released but I was given papers stating that I was 'physically unfit' for National Service. I questioned this document, since on entry to the Air Force I had been declared physically A1, and suggested that perhaps 'mentally unfit' would be more appropriate. To my amazement, I was told that they had deliberately avoided any mention of insanity since they did not want me to have difficulty in obtaining a job in Civvy Street.

RITA

My parents remained married until I was fifteen. At that point my mother fell in love with Julian, a defrocked French priest. He was just a few years older than me and he proposed jokingly that I should call him 'Step'. He taught French for a living and he considered himself to be a writer. When asked what he wrote, he would reply that he was a writer of aphorisms. As a sole form of writing this is certainly nothing of which to be especially proud.

My mother and Julian lived in two rooms on Rosslyn Hill in Hampstead. They had little money and could not possibly afford a country cottage. So, rather enterprisingly, they bought a fishing boat in France. The boat was moored in the harbour of Concarneau in Brittany. The engine had been sold off long before. The boat cost a mere £100. I went to stay with Rita and Step on several occasions during my holidays. We frequently ate mussels that clung to the hull and it was my task to swim around the boat and scrape these into a bucket. At the bottom of the quay there was a superb baker and next door a shop that sold draught cider. These, together with the mussels, provided an excellent meal at practically no cost.

The bunks on the boat were exceedingly uncomfortable. Julian hit on the idea of persuading a nearby bicycle shop to give him their old inner tubes. These he would cut in half and nail across the bunk in place of springs.

After some seven years, in 1956, my mother split up with Julian and it was the least acrimonious divorce imaginable. I offered her the mews flat in which I had been living. It was called Belsize Court Garages. Occasionally I would spend the night in the wood-panelled loft of the mews and Rita would bring me breakfast in bed. If I had a girlfriend with me she was all the more delighted. My mother loved the mews and stayed there almost to the end of her life. She always had a strong preference for younger (much younger) men. There are many 'Rita stories'. One of my favourites dates back to when she was in her late sixties. One day she confessed to my mother-in-law that she was on the pill. My mother-in-law responded: 'Rita, don't be ridiculous.' Whereupon my mother answered: 'But you never know.'

In winter my mother always carried skis on the roof of her car and would take every opportunity of using them. She was passionate about sports of all kinds and taught me from the age of six to play tennis and table tennis, to ice-skate and to ski. On one occasion she was driving south after a trip to Scotland. She left early and drove while it was still dark into a ditch off the motorway. Though she came to no harm, the car was a write-off. Naturally this constituted 'dangerous driving': a court case followed and my mother appeared before the judge who declared, 'I don't think much of your driving, Mrs Masseron.' Rita announced confidently that the contrary was the case. She had in fact been driving especially well on the occasion, she announced. So much so that she had decided to drive through the night. The fact that she had fallen asleep at the wheel could surely not be held against her. The result of all this was that she was not convicted. The judge obviously realized that Rita was totally sincere.

I remember my mother installing a tiny electric stove about

two feet wide and one and a half feet deep in the kitchen of Belsize Court Garages. On this she cooked many hundreds of meals and from time to time she would have a party, producing dinner for as many as forty or fifty. It was close to a miraculous performance. Downstairs in one of the two garages she put up a full-size ping-pong table. It provided constant activity. First she played with me and then with my children Hannah, Alice and Ben, each of whom she had taught. Finally, when well into her eighties, she began to lose her sight until she was almost blind. Even then she continued to play table tennis. Amazingly and triumphantly, she would win the odd point.

Rita lived happily in the mews for thirty years and then at eighty-eight she began to lose her keys repeatedly. In addition, the stairs had become too steep for her. We felt that an old people's home would be more suitable but did not know how to put the idea to her. Finally we managed to persuade her that she was going into a country hotel. This she accepted cheerfully. We had a small scare when she proposed that three of her fellow inmates should visit Belsize Court Garages. Whilst we had left all of Rita's furniture in place, my daughter Alice had moved into the mews and we feared that my mother might recognize the odd alien possession. Fortunately she changed her mind about the visit. Meanwhile she decided upon a far more exciting plan: she signed up a dozen residents of the home, totally ignoring the fact that seven of them were on Zimmer frames, to form a skiing party.

Rita was ninety-one and I had just returned from France. Within five minutes of my reaching the office my son Ben rang to say that she had been admitted to hospital. It was 2 p.m. and I made for the Royal Free Hospital immediately. There I found all three of my children. They travel a great deal and it seemed characteristic of Rita to have chosen a day when we could all be with her. We took it in turns to sit at her bedside. She was barely conscious. And then at 11 p.m. she died.

MY FATHER

My father is important to this story because he was a publisher. In Germany he had earned enough money as a book salesman to buy first one small publishing house and then another. These were called respectively Axel Junker Verlag and Williams Verlag. Axel Junker published dictionaries and Williams was a literary house. The star author was Erich Kästner. There were two other important authors on the backlist, namely Karel Čapek and Kurt Tucholsky. When Hitler came to power my father founded Atrium Verlag in Switzerland to replace Williams Verlag and he transferred his activities to the new publishing house. From Switzerland he continued to sell the books he published and which were banned in Germany and Austria. A brave and even a foolhardy act.

Kästner was perhaps the most popular writer in Germany. He was known as an author of children's books, including *Emil and the Detectives*, and also of adult books, notably

Fabian. In addition he wrote books of poems which sold by the hundreds and thousands of copies. By an extraordinary coincidence, when I arrived at Cape I found that we had for very many years been Kästner's British publisher.

As a child I met Kästner on a number of occasions but cannot say that I liked him. I doubt whether he liked me either. I found the important role he seemed to play in my father's life disturbing. It wasn't simply a case of admiration on my father's part. He idolized the man – so much so that I felt my father was diminished in the process. Kästner drank nothing but champagne and I recall accompanying my father to a bar where his author consumed several bottles. My father had to pay for them of course and being a puritanical man it must have pained him – he would even regard buying a modestly priced bottle of wine for himself as an enormous extravagance. Although he could, on occasion, be generous, he was frequently mean. He would go from shop to shop to find the cheapest strawberries. This tended to result in his buying a punnet with a rotten lower layer of berries. But he had the satisfaction of having saved 2p.

I learned of a particular piece of financial 'caution' on his part when I was hitchhiking around America and visited an old friend of my father's from Vienna. Knowing I had virtually no money, this man offered to give me some, mentioning that he had $5,000 belonging to my father. I declined of course, but when I returned to England I asked my father what the money was intended for. He said he kept it in America in case of 'hard times'.

For my twenty-first birthday my father gave me a duty-free carton of 200 cigarettes. Yet when I needed a substantial sum to buy Jonathan Cape shares that were on offer to me, he did not hesitate to write out a cheque for £5,000. Unlike my mother, he was always 'sensible'. If I looked tired (even whilst I was in my twenties), he would ask when I had gone to bed the previous night, and I might say 2 a.m. It was idiotic of me to tell him the truth. Invariably he would then ask what I had done between midnight and 2 a.m. that I could not have done equally well between 10 p.m. and midnight. When I allowed more than a week to pass without phoning him he would ring me and say, 'Are you all right?' or some such thing. A delay of two weeks would call forth the possibility of death, mine, or even worse, his. And when things got really bad between us, my father would write to me at considerable length. If he expected an answer I invariably disappointed him.

After the war relations with Kästner were resumed but on a less intimate basis. Now my father needed to make a living in England and he had an excellent idea. This was to produce a series of low-priced art books, thus filling a surprising gap in the market. Each book had a dozen plates and was devoted to one of the indisputable 'greats': Toulouse-Lautrec, Cézanne, Degas, and so on. Every book contained an introduction by one of our leading art historians. Being a foreigner and, furthermore, without any money at all, my father needed an English partner. This is where his brilliance showed. After examining the field he decided to approach a most conservative publishing house and one of great quality, Faber and Faber. His encounters at Faber led to the formation of a company called FAMA: FA for Faber and MA for Maschler. Not bad for a refugee. And FAMA was to publish the art-book series which in turn was called 'The Faber Gallery'. Total sales far exceeded a million copies.

The man my father dealt with at Faber was Richard de la Mare, son of the famous poet Walter de la Mare. He took a great pride in his relations with de la Mare. There was just one thing however, that really irritated my dad. On a number of occasions, de la Mare had said, 'You must come and visit us in the country.' He probably meant it but he never actually got round to inviting my father. Such an invitation would have given him tremendous satisfaction. It would have represented ultimate acceptance by an English gentleman.

As a sideline my father founded a Christmas card company. The principal artist was the Czech painter Walter Trier, known in England for his *Lilliput* covers. My father had commissioned Trier to illustrate all Kästner's children's books and he knew him well. Manufacturing Christmas cards was easy and also profitable. The art lies in selling them. And so my father persuaded my mother (they had long been divorced) to take to the road. She found herself driving 50,000 miles a year with a boot full of Christmas cards. Most customers adored her, but a few disliked her so ardently that they would hide in the back of the shop when she entered by the front.

Over the years my father constantly extolled the virtues of being a publisher. By the time I was in my late teens I knew only that whatever profession I chose it would *not* be publishing. And so I went to Rome hoping to pursue a career in films. When I did finally decide to seek a job in publishing my father was jubilant, convinced that he was entirely responsible. I confess that he constantly showed an interest in my career. He especially liked to hear about any powerful figures I got to know: Allen Lane, the founder of Penguin Books, for example. And when I left Penguin to go to Cape, he thought I was crazy: 'How can you leave such an important man and one who thinks well of you?' When I became Managing Director at Cape, five years after joining the company and at the age of thirty-two, I told my father in advance of the announcement and his comment was: 'Haven't they got someone more experienced for the job?' So when, three years later, I was made Chairman, I protected myself by making no mention of it. The appointment was written up in several newspapers and my father read one of the articles. He rang me, terribly hurt, and asked why I had said nothing. I told him.

ROME

My ambition at the age of twenty-two was to become a film director. Given my particular admiration for the Italian Neo-Realist School, I took myself off to Rome. And so, in the autumn of 1955, my train pulled into Stazioni Termini. I had made no arrangements for accommodation, nor did I have a job of any kind. I had not even procured any letters of introduction. However, I did have a destination and that was the Spanish Steps. For me they represented everything that was romantic about Rome. I thought that the immediate vicinity of the Steps would prove too expensive and so I strolled along the Via Due Machelli, which leads off them. Just before the tunnel at the bottom of the street I turned left up the Via Rasella. It is a narrow, unpretentious and little-known street. I was in luck: there I came upon a *pensione* with a tiny two-room apartment vacant at a moderate rent. It was on the fifth floor and without a lift, which probably accounted for the low rent. A balcony looked down upon the street. It was perfect. I installed myself quickly and, filled with excitement, strode back to the Spanish Steps. There I came upon a restaurant called the Taverna Margutta. This happened to be a place frequented by film people and yet the prices were surprisingly reasonable.

At the Taverna Margutta and also at the bar in the Excelsior Hotel (which I had learned was another particular film hang-out) I met two of my heroes: Fellini and De Sica. I asked everyone how I could go about working in Cine Città (the Rome film studios). It seemed strangely difficult. I have often been fortunate in landing jobs that were really tough to obtain but even today I am bemused by the fact that working in the Italian cinema totally defeated me.

Since I wanted to remain in Rome I needed a job. The obvious one was the occupation taken up by most American and English ex-patriates – teaching English. In the *Messagerio* newspaper there were dozens of advertisements every week, many of them inserted by professors from Harvard and Yale, and from Oxford and Cambridge. Price-slashing was fierce. I hit on a ploy which paid surprising dividends. The advertisements were, without exception, written in Italian. I wrote mine in English. And rather than undercutting my rivals I charged approximately three times as much as anyone else. The result was a bonanza. I had many more students than I could possibly take on, and so I was able to pass on a good number to friends.

Like all the other foreign residents, I received my post c/o American Express. One day I came in to collect my letters and I saw a small, stocky figure wearing a black beret. He was leaning against a pillar, clutching a letter, his hand shaking, and with tears rolling down his cheeks. I felt impelled to

approach him with some word of comfort. He simply handed me the damp airmail pages.

The man turned out to be an American poet called Harold Norse. The letter was from a close friend who had been present at a birthday party for Dylan Thomas held in New York. According to the letter, Thomas had given up drinking but then, on his birthday, had started again with a vengeance, so much so that the alcoholic vapours had seeped into his brain cells. He went into a coma and died shortly thereafter. From this encounter I made a close friend – Harold and I would meet at least two or three times a week. He knew many American writers and he lent me their books. I remember being especially taken with the work of Anaïs Nin. She was unknown and unpublished in England at the time.

In addition to educating me, Harold was unwittingly responsible for a tiny act which took on a surprising significance. When the time came for me to return to London he asked whether I would be willing to take a letter to his literary agents, Pearn, Pollinger and Higham, and to post it for him in London since, rightly, he did not trust the Italian mail. Having arrived home, rather than post the letter, I decided to take it in person to the agents' office, and push it through the letterbox, in order to be absolutely certain of its safe delivery. Given my subsequent experience of literary agents, this seems a ridiculously pious act. At the time, it was strangely meaningful.

While writing this book, I visited Isle sur la Sorgue, near Avignon, one Sunday. The village has a weekly antique market and there I ran into a dealer I know. He accosted me: 'I've just been reading about you in the autobiography of an American poet' (he could not remember the poet's name). I had no idea what he was talking about but then I realized that the American poet was Harold Norse. I later discovered that the book was *Memoirs of a Bastard Angel*, first published in New York. It had obviously been translated into French and this was the edition the antique dealer had been reading. I obtained a copy of the American edition and quote from it:

The only person I got to know at the pensione *was a young Englishman called Tom Maschler. Tall, dark, and striking with a mane of straight black hair and keen, aware eyes, he was interested in film-making. My first-hand accounts of Dylan Thomas, Auden and Isherwood impressed him immensely. I said I was broke and he treated me to jelly doughnuts and coffee. He taught English privately and had more students than he could handle. Assuring me that there was plenty of money to be made, he offered me one or two of them. Furthermore, he said, 'They pay a thousand lire apiece.' An immensely cheerful and enthusiastic nineteen [sic].*

Well, I did get one or two students from Tom, but they didn't last. Something else happened that helped me survive. Meanwhile, Tom gave up dabbling in film-making, returned to London and a few years later emerged in his early twenties as the 'wunderkind' of British publishing, the charismatic editor of Jonathan Cape Ltd. In interviews with leading magazines, he attributed his interest in publishing to his meeting with me in Rome. As the first published writer he had met (whilst starving I had given him an inscribed copy of my book The Under Sea Mountain), *I had unknowingly steered him into the literary world, firing his imagination with anecdotes about literary celebrities.*

And so my chance encounter with that French antique dealer took me back to a meeting in Rome that had occurred fifty years previously.

PARIS

MY FIRST VISIT to Paris was in 1950 at the age of seventeen. I fell in love with the city and I have been in love with it ever since. In the early days I made a point of going to hear Juliette Greco sing in a Left Bank basement club. She was a great beauty and chose to perform in the most intimate of venues. At that time it was Edith Piaf the crowds sought out, but for me Greco was the more special.

In the fifties the most famous literary couple in Paris were, without question, Jean-Paul Sartre and Simone de Beauvoir. Whenever I passed the Deux Magots I would take a look inside, just to see whether they were in residence, so to speak. They very frequently were, and although the café is such a public place they always appeared to be totally private and conspiratorial. I never spoke a word to them; that would have been an unthinkable intrusion.

Although contact with Sartre and de Beauvoir was out of the question, I did choose to engineer a meeting with a writer even more private, someone immensely important to me. I knew better than to attempt an encounter by myself. I needed a go-between and I chose the French novelist Robert Pinget, whom I had recently got to know. I asked whether he could arrange a meeting with Samuel Beckett, who was a friend of his. To my surprise Pinget agreed, and some days later I found myself sitting at a terrace café with Beckett and Pinget. Beckett

said hardly anything. It may be that he said nothing at all.
Pinget was almost equally silent. I felt like an intruder and
sensed I was being taught a lesson. And then Beckett got up
and mumbled something as he departed. I watched his lanky
figure stroll down the Boulevard Saint-Germain until it disappeared. Pinget followed and I was left alone and ashamed.

I went to visit Jêrome Lindon at Éditions de Minuit. He
seemed to me the epitome of an intellectual: tall, proud,
intelligent and somewhat arrogant. If a publisher can invent a
literary genre, Lindon invented the *nouveau roman*: Michel
Butor, Nathalie Sarraute, Claude Simon. Lindon had not heard
of me and I doubt whether he had heard of Jonathan Cape
either. He talked about his writers and then he took a number
of books off the shelves which he piled into my arms. Naturally
I did not read everything he gave me, but I did read *L'Herbe*
by Claude Simon and rang to say that I would like to publish

it. I felt that he was surprised and I must admit that I was also, but I had found reading Simon immensely elating. *L'Herbe*, which was published as *The Grass* in England, proved impossibly difficult to sell, but that appeared not to matter. It was a book one *had* to publish, and I went on to publish several further novels by Claude Simon. When I stopped, it was not simply for financial reasons. I must confess that his work had begun to bore me. In 1985 Claude Simon won the Nobel Prize for Literature. It was not long after we had ceased to publish him.

I happened to be in Paris at the time of the publication of *Bonjour Tristesse*. I was invited to a party for the author, a very young girl called Françoise Sagan. I spent a good deal of time talking to her and was strangely fascinated. As I left, someone gave me a copy of *Bonjour Tristesse*, which I put into my suitcase. I thought no more about it until I returned to England. When I unpacked my bag I found the novel. I began to read it and was immediately delighted by the extraordinary economy of the writing. It was most special and controlled, particularly considering the youth of the author. I rang the French publisher right away. I was told that John Murray, a small and rather conservative publisher, had bought the British rights. Later I learned that *Bonjour Tristesse* had taken off in a very big way and Françoise Sagan became a celebrity within weeks. Naturally I kicked myself for having been so slow.

I saw Françoise Sagan again on two further occasions. One was in Saint-Tropez where she was staying together with her *bande*, a group of chic French friends including Brigitte Bardot. It was the only occasion on which I met Bardot and she was even more attractive than I had expected. The second meeting was later in Paris when Sagan's friend Guy Scholler, the head of Hachette, invited me to join the two of them for dinner. Although she remained a celebrity for very many years, Sagan's writing career was disappointing. It is quite common for an author who has an outstanding success with a first book to find it difficult to live up to it later on.

A piece of a non-literary nature. I was invited by Cécile de Rothschild to spend a weekend at her country house just outside Paris. It was my first ever stay in a grand house. Dinner consisted of seven courses. The food was not exactly what I was used to but I could not fail to be impressed. Years later I discovered that the chef was the very young Michel Roux. My undoing was not the food, it was the wines. A different wine was served with each course. After the fourth course I excused myself and made for the lavatory. I got down on my knees and threw up in the bowl. I remember looking into the mirror to see what kind of shape I was in before returning to the dinner table. In the morning I opened the shutters on to a brilliantly sunny day and there, walking across the lawn, was the clearly recognizable figure of Cecil Beaton wearing one of his famous broad-brimmed hats.

Another chance meeting occurred when I was being driven by Monique Lange in her 2CV. Monique ran the Rights Department at Gallimard and was one of my best friends in Paris. We were chattering away and had reached Place de la Concorde. She suddenly shouted out, 'There is Jean. We must stop,' which, in the middle of the Place de la Concorde is

almost an impossibility. But Monique managed it and she went on to attract the attention of Jean, who turned out to be Jean Genet. He climbed into the car and Monique took him off in the direction he was headed. In those days my French was not so hot and Genet spoke exceedingly fast. So the full joy of meeting this unusual writer escaped me. Monique later explained that her excitement at seeing him stemmed from the fact that they had been unable to meet for several months. He had been serving one of his periodic prison sentences.

PART TWO

MY FIRST JOB IN PUBLISHING

AFTER FAILING TO GET anywhere as a film director I decided that I would after all try publishing. And I thought my best chance would be with a small or medium-sized publishing house where I might learn something regardless of my lowly position. The house I focused on was André Deutsch and I was thrilled to be granted an interview by A.D. (as he was called) himself. He was quick to tell me that he had no job to offer. I, in turn, told him that 'Money was no object.' At that he asked when I could start. We settled for the following Monday. As for payment, André proposed what he called a 'Christmas bonus' (there were ten weeks to go until Christmas). And he would then pay me according to what he thought I had been worth. I could not resist pointing out that since he did not plan to pay me any salary at all a 'Christmas bonus' could not possibly count as a 'bonus'. In the event, at Christmas I received a princely £25.

My greatest ambition at Deutsch was to be allowed to attend an editorial meeting. This was never granted. Clearly André did not think me worthy of such an honour. Instead, I was given a number of menial jobs, the most responsible of which was to keep a record of paper stocks. Despite my lowly position I was expected to turn up on Saturdays. Last thing each Friday afternoon A.D.'s cheery voice would seek me out with a 'See you tomorrow.' And believe it or not, when

I turned up, which I did from time to time, he would take the opportunity of bumming cigarettes off me, his excuse being that he had given up smoking and therefore found himself without. My only solution was to follow suit and so I claimed to have given up also. André's meanness, which extended far beyond smoking my cigarettes and placing 20-watt bulbs in the lavatory, irritated me the more in the light of his numerous Savile Row suits and his beautifully manicured hands.

The reader at Deutsch was Francis Wyndham. He was immensely kind and ever ready to educate me. Francis had taken several young writers under his wing, including Bruce Chatwin, all of whose books I was to publish at Cape. Francis read new manuscripts and he also looked after some of the important Deutsch authors, one of whom was Jean Rhys, whose letters he edited. Later, when Francis wrote fiction himself, I felt honoured that he entrusted the publication of his two short novels to me. Francis had the tiniest office I have ever seen. It was there that I dropped in to hand him a little manuscript an acquaintance of mine had bought for a shilling in a junk shop. It was a short (100 pages or so) unpublished typescript, bound in red leather. The author was Virginia Stephen. I recall that on reading the book I had the feeling it was written by a young person. I told Francis that I had been moved by it. He read my offering overnight and was impressed. He congratulated me on my perspicacity while at the same time putting me to shame by pointing out that Virginia Stephen was of course the maiden name of Virginia Woolf. He asked if he could show the manuscript to Deutsch. I declined, just for the hell of it. Instead I returned the book to its owner. Subsequently I lost track of him and of it.

Deprived as I was of my editorial meetings, there were compensations. Vidia Naipaul arrived at the office from time to time and I still cherish the early signed editions of his books which I acquired. I read Naipaul avidly and *A House for Mister*

Biswas remains one of my favourite novels of recent decades. In those days Vidia was only marginally less grumpy than he is today. Laurie Lee, on the other hand, who had just written a book of poems called *My Many-coated Man*, was ever cheerful and friendly. *Cider with Rosie* was still some years off, and by then he had left Deutsch. Another person I remember vividly was Len Deighton, who designed catalogue covers and also book jackets for André. This was the very same man who went on to become one of the most admired British thriller writers. Later I became Len's publisher and am proud of the fact that when he left Hodder & Stoughton after the publication of *The Ipcress File* he chose to go to Cape.

At that time I got to know a young man called Colin Wilson, who used to hang about in my favourite coffee-house. Colin had just completed his book *The Outsider* and he gave me a copy of the manuscript to read. I was fascinated that such a young man should have read so much philosophy. He was able to express his ideas with admirable clarity, so his book was both fascinating and a joy to read. Colin asked me whether I thought he should offer the book to Deutsch. Given my feelings about Deutsch, I suggested he go to another publisher. He went to Gollancz and *The Outsider* became an enormous success.

After Christmas André offered me the job of production manager. I pointed out that I knew nothing about production. André replied that he was confident I could do it 'better than that idiot' (my predecessor). 'That idiot's' salary was £8 per week. André offered me £6. This was so derisory that I decided to run some ski tours and did so from André's office. I even printed a little brochure of which I was rather proud and arranged for my clients to be serviced by Ingham's, one of the most successful ski travel agencies of the day. It was not until after I had left Deutsch that André discovered my treachery.

After three months I presented André with an ultimatum. Unless he paid me £8 forthwith I would leave. André asked me to sleep on it and to come and see him the following day. I said there was no need to sleep on it. He insisted and so I did, but of course I didn't change my mind. André's parting words were that I was a bright boy but, unfortunately, unrealistic about money. My problem, according to André, was that I imagined I would be earning as much as £12 a week in another year or two. He was right.

MacGIBBON & KEE

WHILE WORKING AT Deutsch I had joined the Society of Young Publishers. There I befriended a man called James Clarke who knew a man who had just bought a small, quality publishing house called MacGibbon & Kee. The owner was looking for a young editor and my new friend recommended me. I was interviewed and I got the job. The owner was Howard Samuel, a multi-millionaire and socialist, a friend of Aneurin Bevan and Michael Foot. He also owned the newspaper *Tribune*. More spectacularly, he owned much of Portland Place and numerous other important properties. Unlike many tycoons of today, Howard Samuel loved books and bought the publishing house because he felt it would give him pleasure.

From my point of view, Howard was a model employer. In my two years with MacGibbon & Kee there were just two books of consequence on which I was not given my head. One of them was a novel which earned the label 'a working-class book'. I was so infatuated with it that it seemed important to discuss some revisions I had in mind with the author face to face. His name was Alan Sillitoe and he lived in Majorca. So I went off to see him at my own expense. The cheapest way was by train to Barcelona and then by boat. Spotting my author puffing his pipe as he waited for me on the quay remains a vivid memory. My enthusiasm notwithstanding, we ultimately turned the book down. It was called *Saturday Night and Sunday Morning* and became an instant bestseller. Then, as a result of Karel Reisz's superb film, it went on to sell many hundreds of thousands more copies.

The second book I was obliged to turn down was a most unusual work. The title was *Bang to Rights* and the author was Frank Norman, a thief who had spent a good deal of time in gaol. He had no idea of spelling or grammar and the book contained a great deal of rhyming slang. It had real quality. I wanted to be helpful to Frank and so I sent the manuscript to Stephen Spender. I had a hunch he might like it, and beyond that it occurred to me that he might wish to reprint an extract in *Encounter*, the magazine he edited. That is precisely what happened, and then Secker & Warburg, who distributed *Encounter*, took the book on for publication.

Obviously, my not having been able to publish Sillitoe was a great disappointment. On the other hand, shortly thereafter, I was given a totally free hand to publish a book that I had dreamed up. My idea was to commission a series of manifestos from leading writers in the arts. The subject, inspired to some degree by John Osborne's play *Look Back in Anger*, which had recently transformed the British theatre, was the manner in which we might affect our society. My contributors included Doris Lessing, Kenneth Tynan, John Osborne and Colin Wilson. We called the book *Declaration*. I was so closely identified with it that I was even allowed to art-direct the jacket. I wanted an unusual and powerful image and approached Eduardo Paolozzi, who was already considered one of our leading sculptors. Paolozzi agreed and to me this seemed something of a coup. It was by no means as easy to persuade my contributors to participate. John Osborne was especially hesitant but his essay turned out to be one of the best. Without his contribution we would never have had that memorable definition of our Queen. He called her 'the gold filling in a mouthful of decay'.

I contributed a short introduction, and wherever the book was reviewed (which was almost everywhere), there appeared the by-line 'edited by Tom Maschler', which of course gave me a sense of pride. The reviews surpassed my wildest dreams. Two of our leading critics, Philip Toynbee and Cyril Connolly, wrote at great length and with considerable enthusiasm in the *Observer* and the *Sunday Times* respectively. This resulted in a hardcover sale of some 20,000 copies, which is an enormous number for a book of essays. *Declaration* was translated into French, German, Italian, Spanish and Japanese. The fact that I did not earn a penny from the book in no way detracted from the satisfaction it gave me.

Shortly after the publication of *Declaration*, Howard Samuel asked me into his office. He seemed distinctly nervous as he delivered his message. 'I do not in the least mind you giving press interviews. I do not even mind you giving the impression that you are running the company. But I would prefer it if you did not give the impression that you also owned it.' This was the only reprimand I ever received from Howard and I felt a sense of shame. If I had given this impression I most certainly had not done so deliberately. It seemed to me a confirmation of the fact that I have always found it difficult to see myself as an employee. One day I mentioned that I was thinking of buying a house, and Howard offered to come and look at it with me. We went together to Chalcot Crescent and he declared that it was on the edge of a slum and therefore he must advise against. I said, 'But it is just at the foot of Primrose Hill.' He did not change his view but I decided to go ahead none the less. The house cost £1,400. The last house to be sold in that street went for over £1,200,000. Obviously there is a fifty-year gap but such a multiple is exceptional.

PENGUIN BOOKS

FOR ME THE PUBLICATION of *Declaration* had the most
unexpected consequence. At that time Allen Lane, the founder
of Penguin Books, had decided to hire one or two young
people. The response to *Declaration* gave him the idea that its
editor might be a suitable person and he invited me to come
and see him. Now, to my mind Penguin Books was the greatest
publishing innovation of our time. Penguin had a unique
quality which, alas, the company has lost today. The quality to
which I refer rests primarily in the books they published.
Penguin were the first in the paperback field and so they had
the greatest possible choice of titles. They also designed their
books immaculately and invariably gave them a 'classy' look.
Allen Lane offered me the position of Assistant Fiction Editor,
working under Eunice Frost. I derived a particular satisfaction
from the fact that he was ready to pay me approximately four
times as much as I had earned *chez* Deutsch.

This happy news from Penguin came at the same time as a
very sad event. During the summer holiday with his family,
Howard Samuel had walked into the sea and disappeared. No
one knew exactly what happened. It did not make sense, but it
was thought that he committed suicide. We were certainly not
close – he was a man who kept himself at a distance from
almost everyone – and yet I felt as though I had lost a good
friend.

Eunice Frost had been with Allen Lane since the beginning, when he founded Penguin in a crypt. From the day I joined until the day I left, two years later, Eunice never spent a single day in the office; I don't know whether it provides some sort of explanation, but she had just got married. And so, aged twenty-five, I did her job as well as mine. I was solely responsible for buying the paperback rights to some seventy or eighty novels a year. At this point I did not have a single reader to help me, and to make matters worse, for the most part I was unfamiliar with the previous books of most of the authors in question. My image of a Penguin book was a 'good' book. Just that. So when, for example, a new Angela Thirkell came along, I turned it down. This resulted in the publisher telephoning Allen Lane to ask what was going on. He always backed me up. Despite all his publishing genius he was not a great reader himself since he had no strong opinion of his own, and was therefore the more ready to accept my view.

I did not greatly enjoy reprint publishing. The problem was that whilst one could easily follow suit if a book had been a success in hardcover, when a book had failed it was extremely difficult to make a mark with the paperback. One fiction area from which I derived particular satisfaction because it had been relatively neglected was that of European literature. Here I was on familiar ground and I enjoyed myself buying the works of such great writers as Thomas Mann and Albert Camus.

Prior to my arrival, Penguin had never published an original work of fiction. I decided to focus my attention on one particular area, namely drama. At that time the Penguin theatre list was made up of the likes of George Bernard Shaw, Christopher Fry and Terence Rattigan. This was as modern as it went. The drama editor was a man called Martin E. Browne. He was also a director and had directed, for example, the plays of T. S. Eliot. He was, as you may imagine from the publishing programme, on the conservative side. One day I asked him why we did not publish any modern playwrights. His answer astonished me: 'Are there any?' And this was after the advent of John Osborne's *Look Back in Anger* which, in addition to creating a revolution in the theatre, had spawned many new playwrights. I offered to lend Martin Browne some sample plays. In those days I followed the theatre closely and especially the Royal Court Theatre. I happened to have three scripts at home. They were *Chicken Soup with Barley* by Arnold Wesker, *The Hamlet of Stepney Green* by Bernard Kops, and *To Each His Own Wilderness* by Doris Lessing. These three I handed to Martin as evidence of 'new plays'.

Next time I saw him I asked immediately, 'What did you think?'

'They are awfully good,' he replied, to my surprise. 'Why don't we publish them?'

And so we did. With an eye to the future I came up with a series title, *New English Dramatists*. The staggering fact is that the very first volume sold over 200,000 copies. The book was published as 'edited by Martin E. Browne'. Everyone at Penguin was amazed by our success and wanted further volumes. These I put together. At the same time I asked Martin whether he would mind if my name appeared as editor! He looked a bit taken aback but raised no objection.

There was another opportunity for innovation at Penguin.

This time it was Allen Lane's idea. He had the notion of publishing a series of non-fiction science books that would be heavily and graphically illustrated, and in colour. Allen had decided that the most suitable artists for such a project could be found in Switzerland and he invited me to join him on a scouting trip to Zurich.

It was an exciting prospect. I do not know what got into me but I took it into my head to drive to Heathrow in my old car, a convertible Sunbeam Alpine, on the day of our journey. The car refused to start. When it finally did so I knew that I was unlikely to make it to the airport in time for our plane. Allen held the tickets and throughout my car journey I was speculating what my boss would do. Finally I rushed into check-in, and there he stood, perfectly calm, with those narrow and unusually cold lips, the white cuffs of his shirt protruding as they always did. I was bursting to explain myself but he cut me short. 'Don't say a thing. We all live in terror of missing an airplane and nobody would do so except by accident.' I was, and still am, filled with admiration.

I believe that Allen had taken a liking to me early on or at least that there was something about me that intrigued him. Either way, he invited me frequently to Silverbeck, his country house, for dinner or the weekend. The house was located close to Harmondsworth and hence convenient for the office. It was there that Allen kept his signed copies of all Penguins. Thousands of them.

On one occasion I was invited to a big party. What happened was totally uncharacteristic of this apparently unemotional man. One of the guests from abroad was my favourite German publisher, Ledig Rowohlt. He arrived with his mistress of long standing, Susanne Lepsius. Allen took a fancy to Susanne. She stayed on with him the following day when Rowohlt returned to Germany and she remained, as Allen's mistress, for many years thereafter. Meanwhile, Allen's wife departed for Germany together with Rowohlt. This did not last very long.

I had been at Penguin for a year and a half when I asked Allen whether, if Eunice was never going to show up, I might be officially appointed as Fiction Editor. He refused, saying that he did not want to hurt her feelings. I found his reply disappointing. But that apart, I did not find working at Penguin satisfying. And so, when Michael Howard (the son of Bob Wren Howard) approached me as to whether I would be interested in the position of Literary Director of Jonathan Cape, I said I would. Shortly thereafter the job was formally offered to me and I accepted. Allen Lane was not simply upset. He was furious. How could I leave when I had such a great future at Penguin? He even said that he had been thinking of me as his successor. I strongly suspect that he had said something similar to one if not two other people.

DISCOVERING AMERICA

I JOINED CAPE in May 1960. Jonathan Cape had died one month previously and I enormously regret that I never met him. My boss and co-founder of the company, Bob Wren Howard, suggested that I should continue the company tradition of making annual trips to New York. Over the years, as a result of Jonathan's New York visits, Cape had come to publish a good number of American authors, including Ernest Hemingway, Eugene O'Neill and one 'younger' writer, Irwin Shaw, who was not in fact all that young, whom I had the pleasure of taking under my wing. He lived in New York and Klosters.

In preparation for my trip I asked Jonathan's secretary, Jean Mossop, who still worked for us, to let me have a list of the publishers and agents Jonathan used to visit. I thought it a good plan to introduce myself so that I might benefit from old contacts. However, I found that the majority of those on her list were either dead or retired, so I made my own enquiries. The single publisher whose name came up most frequently and with whom over the years I have found myself compared (indeed, we have been called terrible twins) was Bob Gottlieb. The most 'special' agent was Candida Donadio. Neither of these featured on Jonathan's list but they became the two individuals with whom I worked most intensely over many years.

I first met Bob Gottlieb in his office at Simon and Schuster. Lunch was something he virtually never indulged in. He considered it a waste of time. This is an attitude I too have adopted over the years. I make an exception only for the celebration of an author's publication day and even then I have a strong preference for dinner. Bob held forth on a number of favourite books and authors and I took pages of notes. We liked each other immediately. Subsequently Bob invited me to stay at his home and I did so for some twenty years in a row.

Once I took a taxi from the airport to Bob's house and found on arrival that I had hardly any money. I wasn't worried because I knew that Bob was well off and could lend me the fare. I cheerfully asked him for it and he said he had no cash whatsoever. This made little sense to me but Bob explained that Americans use credit cards for everything. The only cash in Bob's house was thousands of pennies (100 to the dollar) which were kept in an enormous glass jar, and he collected for charity. The taxi driver was not best pleased.

My staying with Bob greatly cemented our friendship. There are always snags to staying with friends and at the risk of it sounding ridiculous I will tell this story. It was my very first visit. Having arrived on the night flight, I felt like having a boiled egg for breakfast. There were no eggs to be found in the kitchen and I cheerfully went out to a nearby deli. I returned carrying a dozen eggs to discover, unlikely as it may sound, that there was no salt. Back to the deli. Food does not play a significant part in Bob's life. His wife, Maria Tucci, is a successful American actress and she is an extremely good cook but often working. In the interim Bob will happily consume ice-cream for dinner. He eats it straight from the carton and frequently while standing up in the kitchen.

For me the most rewarding part of staying *chez* Gottlieb

was the talks we had after I returned from an evening out for dinner. I invariably found Bob on his bed, propped against enormous pillows and devouring a vast pile of manuscript. He was always eager to learn what I had been up to and equally eager to tell me what I should have been doing. With the possible exception of Sonny Mehta, who happened to become Bob's successor, Bob was the only American publisher I admired almost without reservation. One of the reasons I so much enjoyed our talks at his house was that I found it absolutely impossible to speak to him at the office. There he pursued his passion frantically and relentlessly. He had a team of people, of course, and he pretended to defer to them, but in reality it was Bob who took all the decisions. Although I did not like his style in this respect I must admit that at times he reminded me of myself. Bob always wore sneakers in the office and he invariably looked scruffy. That was his style.

At Bob's house we discussed endlessly all the elements of our profession. We even had time to gossip. And so Bob told me a delightful story. He had recently received a phone call from his neighbour, whose garden backed on to his. The person in question was Katharine Hepburn. She was calling to say that there had been a particularly heavy snowfall in the night. She had immediately swept her roof so that the snow would not melt and create a leak, and was urging Bob to do

the same. He replied that he did not even know how to find the trapdoor to his roof. Thereupon she offered to come over and sweep Bob's roof for him. Katharine Hepburn was in her seventies at the time.

One day when I was staying with Bob I came down to the kitchen at 5 a.m., badly jetlagged, to make a cup of tea. The front door opened and 'Nica' (Nicolo Tucci), the father of Bob's wife, Maria, and a writer I had published, walked in. He made a habit of strolling about the city in the very early morning and would take the opportunity of letting himself into the house and raiding his daughter's fridge. He looked at me and said, 'What are you doing here? You can easily afford a hotel.' I think that was the last time I stayed with Bob and Maria.

In the case of Candida Donadio the sympathy was even more striking. It was almost love at first sight. I do not mean physical love. It was Candida's spirit that was so seductive; even at our very first meeting we talked non-stop in her office all afternoon. She invited me to dinner later in the week. She was almost witchlike in her perception of literature. We never discussed business when we met. We left that for correspondence or the telephone.

*

ON AVERAGE I had about eight appointments a day including breakfast, lunch and dinner, and so in two weeks I met close on a hundred publishing people. I don't think I ever worked so hard in my life. At the end of my first week in New York I received a letter from Michael Howard. He was at pains to give me the news before I heard it from elsewhere. There was a plan for the three key people at Michael Joseph, Peter Hebden, Charles Pick and Roland Gant, to join Cape. The architect of this plan and also the main backer was Allen Lane. He undertook to purchase Jonathan Cape's shares.

I had known that these shares would have to be sold for the Cape family to be able to pay the necessary death duties. I rang Michael Howard immediately. My first question was to ask where I stood under this arrangement. I found it quite extraordinary but Michael told me that I had not been discussed at all. I pointed out that if the deal went ahead my position would almost certainly be in jeopardy. He seemed surprised. I thought of returning to London right away but decided to stay another week and complete my business. I have often been asked what made me stay on when the temptation to catch the first plane back in order to attempt to save the situation was so great. I can only say that some instinct made me determined to complete the work that I had planned. I knew I was on to some important books.

By the time I returned news of the deal had leaked into the press. It sounded very much more definite than I had been led to believe. On my first day back in the office, I requested that

I should be present at the next meeting with 'The Trinity', as Wren Howard called them. Michael thought this might be difficult to arrange but I was insistent. And so I went to see Michael's father, who agreed immediately. I might add that I took the opportunity of telling him that in the event of my being pushed out it would not be long before he and Michael were also out.

The crucial meeting took place the third day after my return. Wren Howard was in the chair and began by asking 'The Trinity' to declare their position with regard to me. Peter Hebden acted as spokesman and said, 'I am sorry to have to say this in front of you, Tom, but you must go.' Wren Howard simply announced that there was no more to be said and he closed the meeting. It was over within minutes. The door shut and the three departed. Michael's father clapped his hands and said, 'That's that.' At this stage virtually none of the books I had bought had been published. My chances of survival seemed practically nil. You may imagine the gratitude I felt. Wren Howard showed a staggering sense of loyalty and confidence. To back me when I had only just joined the company was extraordinary, especially since I was up against three enormously experienced old-handers.

Even after 'The Trinity' had been disposed of, the problem regarding the sale of Jonathan Cape's shares remained. It was Sidney Bernstein who bought the shares and so came to the rescue. I had never met Sidney and knew only his reputation as a tough businessman. He turned out to be the very opposite in my case. Sidney was so pleased with our performance that he offered to sell me, and also Graham Greene, approximately 10 per cent of his holding. The value of the shares was now substantially more than it had been when Sidney bought the shares and yet he sold them to us at well below the price he had himself paid. I have always felt that this was an extraordinary piece of generosity and it led to something of a friendship between us.

Once I recovered from my narrow escape I began to sort through my notes. I started with the most copious, taken during my meetings with Bob Gottlieb. In a letter to Bob, I ran through the books on which he said he would give us first offer and then those about which he had a particular hunch and those on which he offered to keep me informed. And so my letter went on until finally I wrote: 'and now, I have this idiot note which says "*Catch 18*" and, in brackets, "sold to Secker & Warburg". Why did I write that when the book was sold?'

Bob replied right away. American publishers are on the whole inordinately slow correspondents and Bob is a rare exception. What he said was: 'I imagine you wrote it down because I have been working with the author for ten years and it is the book I am most passionate about. By an extraordinary coincidence we received a letter from Fred Warburg the very day your letter arrived. Fred wrote to say that *Catch 18* was so American that no one in England could possibly understand it. In fact he considered the book unpublishable. And he went on to ask whether we would be willing to release him from his contract.' Bob had, he told me, spoken to Candida (for she was the agent) and they were both agreed that I should have the next offer. A proof was on its way to me via her. The book was of course Joseph Heller's *Catch-22*. We changed the title when Leon Uris published a book called *Mila 18*. I read *Catch-22* overnight and felt ecstatic about it. It is a war book in essence but unlike most celebrated war books it is essentially anti-war. *Catch-22* is also extremely funny, so much so that I frequently laughed aloud as I read it. *Catch-22* is a clause in the army statutes according to which one would be crazy to fly more missions and sane if one did not, but if sane, one had to fly them. And if one flew them, one was crazy and did not have to. We paid the princely advance of £250. *Catch-22* has a unique place in my publishing history. It was the first novel I bought for Cape and it went on to become the most successful American first novel I have published. In the first three months we sold 50,000 copies and even outsold the American edition. For an American author to be more successful in the UK than in the States is virtually unheard of. Bob Gottlieb paid us the compliment of taking a whole-page advertisement in the *New York Times* quoting British reviews and the British success story.

We got behind the book in an unusual way. Tony Colwell, our Promotions Director, produced a sixteen-page brochure for booksellers about the novel and its author. He also commissioned a cartoonist to draw the main characters in the book and underneath each drawing we printed some hilarious quotes from the text itself. Four different cards were inserted in each copy of the book. I sent out proof copies to various friends whom I considered influential. I recall that the first two to respond and to embrace the book were Kenneth Tynan and Edna O'Brien. They were the first of very many.

Joseph Heller followed *Catch-22* with *Something Happened*. This was a 'serious' novel and although less well known and less commercial, it is a work of art. Regina and I got to know Joe, and when he came to England we invariably invited him to dinner. He returned the compliment in East Hampton. I shall never forget the first occasion we were at his home. One bottle of wine (litre size) appeared on the table to be shared among ten guests. There was plenty of whisky, which I do not drink. I observed, not for the first time, that the myth about Americans not drinking wine applies only to Americans in their own homes. I asked Joe if he would mind my going out to buy a few more bottles of wine. He said,

'Not in the least.' And he directed me to the nearest liquor store.

Over the years we have built up a formidable American list. Many were first books and a number of others were by authors who joined us because for one reason or another they were unhappy with their previous British publishers. I am proud of the fact that we have never offered extravagant sums with a view to seducing authors. Take the case of Philip Roth. He had written a book called *When She Was Good*. His publisher, André Deutsch, offered an advance of £3,000 which Philip felt should be £4,000. André declined. We bought the rights for £4,000. I should add that Philip was already much admired among young American authors and furthermore that he had won the National Book Award for his first book. It follows that £4,000 seemed a perfectly reasonable request. The irony, which I'm sure did not escape Deutsch, was that Philip's next book turned out to be *Portnoy's Complaint*. This was a momentous success, even greater than *Catch-22*, and far out-sold any previous Philip Roth novel.

Philip and I became good friends and I would see him regularly, together with various – always pretty – girlfriends in both London and New York. Then he married Claire Bloom and shortly afterwards they invited us to their country house in Connecticut. Our stay was memorable if not altogether pleasant. They had one other houseguest, the American writer Marianne Wiggins. She was deeply embittered by the break-down of her marriage to Salman Rushdie. In the middle of dinner she took it upon herself to launch an attack on me. The charge was that I had the gall to be well off. This was brought on by Claire asking to see photographs of our house in France. Marianne's tirade was as relentless as it was puzzling and Philip and Claire were as embarrassed as I. It would be charitable to say that she was drunk. After dinner, which seemed to last an eternity, I asked Philip to accompany me for a stroll. I told him that I really couldn't drive back to New York together with Ms Wiggins in the taxi he had ordered for us. He pleaded eloquently, saying that there was only one available taxi nearby, and in addition he had, I suspect, promised Marianne that we would share the cost. My friendship with Philip commanded that I capitulate.

In the morning we had another setback. On our arrival the previous night Philip had showed us exactly where to put our luggage – we had just arrived from London and there was a lot of it. He was at pains to explain that the barn roof leaked and so it was important to avoid certain areas. I failed to listen and the next morning our luggage was sodden. Philip took it badly.

In fact he was quite angry. He prides himself on being a good host and is also a man in need of order. Our journey back with Marianne passed tolerably. We drove in total silence and I have no doubt that she had a hangover. That was the last occasion on which I saw Philip. When he and Claire separated he wrote a vindictive book about her, and she wrote a vindictive book about him. Subsequently Philip went into exile and since then he has been writing magnificent book after magnificent book. For once the phrase writing 'at the height of his powers' is justified.

*

WILLIAM STYRON is a good friend of Philip's. He also lives in Connecticut though it is only his winter home. His summers are spent in a most beautiful house set in large grounds on the waterfront in Martha's Vineyard. Styron was already famous when I first met him. His agent, John Dodds, mentioned to me that Bill had not heard from his British publisher, Hamish Hamilton, for several years. He was therefore quite eager to leave them. Dodds went on to say that he thought Styron and I would get on well. Certainly the prospect of publishing Bill excited me enormously. He rarely visited New York and so the best plan, said Dodds, was to go to Martha's Vineyard. I was eager to do so if John would ring Styron to make the introduction. 'I'll tell you what, I'll take you,' said Dodds. 'The airplanes will be booked up [it was summertime] and so I suggest we drive.' I was taken aback by such generosity and asked whether it wasn't rather far to drive. 'It's only eight hours,' said Dodds. So drive we did. And when we got there our meeting was a success and Styron gave me the first hundred pages of *The Confessions of Nat Turner* to take away and read. You may imagine how proud I felt to be offered the opening pages of a new book by such a magnificent writer. I am eternally grateful to John Dodds for the part he played in this.

Styron has several times invited me to stay with him and his wife Rose in Martha's Vineyard. On the first occasion he announced upon my arrival that it was a pity I had not been there the previous day because Marilyn Monroe was staying with them. Styron added in his distracted way, 'Come to think of it, she slept in your room.' Every young man's fantasy almost come true. The following day Styron excused himself and Rose from dinner. They were, he told me, going out with Caroline, or that is how it sounded. They would be leaving at 7 p.m., I was told, and my dinner would be served at 8 p.m. At exactly 7 p.m. I heard a loud rushing sound on the lawn

in front of the house and Bill and Rose scampered into a helicopter. It occurred to me that the helicopter must be the one called *The Caroline*, which belonged to John F. Kennedy. Clearly it was with him that they were having dinner. This was no isolated incident in the life of the Styrons. They were close friends of the Kennedys and of many key American political figures. With such connections it cannot be easy to get much writing done. And so it isn't surprising that it takes Bill many years to complete a new book.

In addition to their political friends, the Styrons know a large number of writers and intellectuals. One of these, who was a particular childhood hero of mine, is Arthur Miller. In my late teens *Death of a Salesman* and *The Crucible* were two of my greatest theatrical experiences. And now, thirty years later, Arthur Miller appeared at Bill and Rose's house in Connecticut. He lived nearby and he had come to play tennis with Rose. I recall the size of his feet which seemed enormous and appeared even bigger in tennis sneakers that were at least a size too large. As for the rest of his clothing, there was no concession to tennis whites. Off the court Miller was relaxed and conversation flowed. A subject of particular interest was the merits of the local grocery store, along with similar topics. For me it was impossible not to think about his marriage to Marilyn Monroe but of course there was no mention of her.

Nat Turner was followed some years later by *Sophie's Choice*, one of the most gripping and wonderful books I have ever published. Although Styron was gracious most of the time, he could be quite taciturn. I was filled with admiration for the way in which his delightful wife Rose coped. She pretended to ignore Bill's moods but the degree of her caring for him was always evident. At one point his moods took him into a serious depression. He wrote a moving book about it called *Darkness Visible*.

A SPECIAL PLACE

MOST PEOPLE WORKING in publishing would concede that from the late sixties to the early eighties Cape was the greatest literary publishing house in England. We had the best authors, we produced the best promotions, and our production was the best. This was so good that Anthony Blond, a small independent publisher, announced in a speech on publishing that instead of employing someone to do a production job he simply made a practice of sending a Cape book to the printer, saying, 'Make it like that.'

We were a team like no other. For both our authors and staff it was thrilling to belong to Cape. We occupied a house in Bedford Square, one of the most beautiful squares in England. As the door of number 30 opened, a sense of excitement and happy anticipation could be felt. It was such a stimulating place that the days were never long enough. People at all levels worked long and unasked-for hours without even being aware of it. Although some of them thought of me as superior, and I must confess I sometimes frightened people, almost everyone called me by my first name. I worked at such a pace that there was no question of my reading even a few manuscript pages in the office. Such things were for the weekends and evenings at home. I recall many years later apologizing to my children for having been such an unsatisfactory father.

For my first seven years at Cape I was in sole charge of all

book acquisitions. Except for new books from Cape authors of the past (and there were very few of those), every book we published was brought in by me. Then I decided to employ an editorial director. My first choice was Ed Victor, then working for Weidenfeld & Nicolson. Ed was a highly intelligent and congenial young American graduate. He stayed with us for a number of years until his wife Micheline won the day by persuading Ed that I was a 'filthy capitalist', and so he left to start an underground magazine together with Richard Neville. Subsequently Ed left Micheline and went on to become one of England's most successful, and wealthy, literary agents.

Replacing Ed was not easy. I chose a literary agent called David Machin. We got on well, but through no one's fault the 'fizz' was missing. It took several lunches and many weeks to persuade Liz Calder to join us from Gollancz. She was clearly one of the best editorial directors in London and I was thrilled when she finally said yes. We worked closely together until Liz was invited to become a founder member of Bloomsbury. This proved irresistible and we lost her.

Even before we took on our first literary director I employed some readers on a part-time basis. I often found that my friends' wives especially enjoyed the job and were particularly good at it. They included Claire Tomalin, wife of my friend Nick Tomalin who was killed in the Golan Heights, and Jane Miller, the wife of Karl Miller.

I felt a sense of pride when Patsy, our wonderful reception-ist, said that she could feel my presence in the building even when she had not seen me enter. Towards the end of the day I made a point of wandering into other offices. There I would often find an author or two who had dropped in for a cup of tea – very much that rather than alcohol. Graham Greene and I led the way. Most days we were the first to arrive (between 8 and 9 a.m.) and the last to leave (between 7 and 8 p.m.). I was enormously proud of the fact that we all shared the same commitment and passion for our work. The one luxury I allowed myself in the office was to hire a yoga teacher, sharing the classes with anyone who wanted to participate. We had a class of twenty or so and I was one of the least adept. We each paid for ourselves but it was a minimal sum. The place felt like a happy family.

At that time the Allen Lane Award was founded. The best

publisher was awarded a heavy brass object some eighteen inches high. The award was for excellence in all its aspects. We won the first year. We did not win the second year. But we won again in the third year and the fourth. Thereupon it was abandoned.

I realize that it is an extravagant claim, but during my thirty years at Cape I doubt whether I spent more than an hour a week doing something I did not actively enjoy. In this respect it was my greatest good fortune that Graham cheerfully undertook all the (to me) arduous tasks: finance, pensions, the sales department, insurance, the production department and, most demanding of all, libel. In addition to all this Graham enjoyed being a director or chairman of various other boards: Director of Greene King, the family brewery, Chairman of the Publishers' Association, Chairman of the British Museum. For my part, with the exception of the Society of Young Publishers when I was very young, throughout my forty years in publishing I have never sat on a single committee. Instead, I spent my energy at Cape entirely on matters editorial and matters promotional. We made a promotional event out of our sales conferences which were rather unlike those of other publishing houses. It seemed essential to me that the books should be presented by those who cared most passionately for them, that is to say by readers and editors (and me) as opposed to salespeople. I believe that the success of a book is created within the publishing house and that if there is enough enthusiasm within the company it will ultimately infect the outside world. Before my time the Cape sales conference was attended only by a narrow publishing circle. I decided to invite everyone in the company, including all secretaries and those who worked at reception.

Graham and I were housed in adjoining rooms, connected by enormous double doors. His office was a little smaller than mine but he had the advantage of looking out on to Bedford

Square. Mine was a little larger but looked on to the back of the building. We never knocked on each other's door but walked freely from office to office. We talked almost exclusively of business matters. From time to time I would tell Graham about some personal aspect of my life. He would tell me virtually nothing of his. Graham's father was Hugh Carlton Greene, Director General of the BBC, and his uncle (Hugh's brother) was the famous writer Graham Greene. Graham's mother, Helga Greene, was a literary agent and it is no great secret that she had a long affair with a hero of mine, Raymond Chandler. But of course Graham never made mention of this.

I was given to understand by Graham's stepmother, Elaine Greene (also a literary agent), that the Greenes are famous (or perhaps notorious) for their secrecy. Here is an example. Once a week Graham and I and three leading colleagues would have lunch at Bertorelli's, an Italian restaurant five minutes' walk from our offices. On one occasion Graham was absent and when we arrived at our usual table there stood a bottle of champagne on ice. A card invited us to drink to Graham and his new (second) spouse. The card informed us that they would be married by the time we reached Bertorelli's. The most galling aspect of this for me was not that Graham might get married without telling me in advance, but that he could get married to someone I had never even met. None the less we worked for a quarter of a century in complete harmony. We trusted each other totally, supported each other at all times, and neither of us ever interfered with the work of the other. Naturally we would consult each other about certain important decisions, but that is as far as it went. Graham was called Managing Director and I was called Chairman. It could just as well have been the other way about. Graham looked after the interests of our staff on a daily basis. I looked after our authors.

We gave an annual party which people were at pains to crash. It was recognized as by far the most enjoyable literary party of the year. We invited no press – we did not want the party to be written up. When *The Times* rang, as they often did, to ask whether they could send a photographer, the answer was a regretful no. We invited people (mainly authors and a few literary agents) because we liked them and for no other reason. Our party had a very special quality, difficult to define. It was mainly the guests who contributed to this, although I think the food also played a part. This was what I would call 'real' food as opposed to caterer's food. The party was always held in early December and quite frequently authors would ask me for the date as early as October since they wanted to be sure not to miss it.

DORIS LESSING

I FIRST MET Doris the day I went to visit her in the hope that she might agree to write an essay for a book I was editing. This was *Declaration*; the subject matter, the thoughts and aspirations of some of our leading writers and critics. At that time the press had decided that anyone aspiring to change society was an 'Angry Young Man'. Doris wrote in her autobiography, *Walking in the Shade*:

> *And now enter Tom Maschler, very young – twenty-three – handsome and ambitious, who arrived in my flat with a demand that I write a piece for a book he planned, called* Declaration. *I said I hated writing think pieces. He said reproachfully that his whole future depended on this book. I later discovered that this was how we all agreed: we could not withstand Tom's need. Besides, he had approached Iris Murdoch – he said – and she said no, and he had to have a woman in it: I could not let him down. This is how I became an 'Angry Young Man'. . . .*
>
> *Tom was for years an enterprising, a brilliant publisher; he brought Jonathan Cape from a moribund condition to being the liveliest publishing house in Britain; he found new authors and cherished and supported them; he fought for books at first patronized or rubbished by reviewers, like* One Hundred Years of Solitude *and* Catch-22; *he has kept his friends loyal to him through thick and thin.*

At the time I was working for MacGibbon & Kee. Having talked Doris into contributing to *Declaration*, I somehow persuaded her to leave the publishing house of Michael Joseph, with whom she had been ever since her first novel, *The Grass Is Singing* (she brought the manuscript with her when she left Rhodesia to come to Britain in 1949). The first book Doris gave me to publish was a volume of short stories called *The Habit of Loving*. I was not to serve Doris well at MacGibbon & Kee, for it was not long thereafter that Allen Lane, founder of Penguin, offered me a job I could not resist. Meanwhile, I am happy to say that Howard Samuel, the property millionaire and owner of MacGibbon & Kee, who much admired Doris's work, offered her, at my suggestion, a flat for a peppercorn rent. So at least I made an indirect contribution to her well-being. I should add that Doris never reproached me for my indecently speedy defection.

During my Penguin period Doris and I continued to see each other regularly. We felt an enormous affection for one another which has lasted a lifetime. Indeed there is no one in my life I value more. Going back to the late fifties, it was Doris I drove to the Black Mountains the day I came to take possession of my beloved cottage, Carney. Many years later, when I could not afford the boarding-school fees for my daughter Hannah, Doris offered without hesitation to pay them. This was to be a gift and not a loan, the only condition being that I must tell no one and least of all Hannah. Such generosity is typical of Doris. I have no doubt that she spends more of her income on others than on herself.

When I started the series of plays called *New English Dramatists* at Penguin, I was able to include Doris's play *To Each His Own Wilderness* in the very first volume. Then, when I went to Cape after two years at Penguin, Doris joined me. I am so much in awe of her work that it was always an enormous pleasure to make a very special effort for each new book, and indeed she was very happy with the way we published her.

Doris has published some fifty books, is translated all over the world, and no doubt earns a great deal. She lives in a modest house in NW6. If you visited her you might imagine you were in the home of a relatively affluent student. And she would not have it otherwise.

The book that is commonly considered Doris's masterpiece is *The Golden Notebook*, published in 1962. It is certainly one of the greatest contemporary novels. The range of Doris's work is extraordinary. She writes at all times in an idiosyncratic and frequently moving manner. In my opinion, she should have won the Nobel Prize in Literature long ago, and what fun she would have giving away the best part of $1,000,000. I am sure that Doris would claim not to care about the prize, but it is I who passionately want her to have it. Thirteen of my authors have won the Nobel Prize and on several occasions I did not even bother to go to Stockholm for the awards ceremony. For Doris to win would be the most marvellous event.

It is a pleasurable bonus when an author recommends the work of another writer to their publisher, although this happens surprisingly rarely. Doris is an exception and has passed on to me several friends and authors. One such was Idries Shah, the Sufi master. Although Doris was for many years a Communist, she subsequently embraced Sufism. And so I came to publish a number of Shah's titles, including theoretical books and several volumes of Nasruddhin tales. These are rather forbiddingly known as 'teaching stories'. But they are a great delight to read.

After more than twenty-five years at Cape I began to spend a good deal of time in France and Doris felt neglected. Doris grew increasingly unhappy and of course she told me so. I felt a sense of despair. There was nothing I could do to compensate for my absence and so Doris left. We have continued to see each other regularly, meeting for dinner frequently, just the two of us, with never a lapse in the conversation. My interest in her and her son Peter, and her interest in me, my wife Regina and in my children, is as strong as it ever was. In the absence of publishing matters, personal relations take on an ever greater importance.

In 2000 Gail Rebuck, the dynamic head of Random House, gave a party to celebrate my forty years with the company. It was held at the Lansdowne Hotel and was a most splendid affair. Among the guests was the Italian publisher Inge Feltrinelli, who had flown in from Milan just for the evening. She stood up in her impassioned way and told of how she had first met me forty years previously at the Frankfurt Book Fair. She was there with her late husband, Giangiacomo Feltrinelli, one of the greatest publishers of our time. Then she said, totally out of context, 'Tom was in love with Doris forty years ago, and he still is.'

ARNOLD WESKER

ARNOLD AND I first met in Coventry in 1958. At the time I was a fanatical theatregoer and very ready to drive a long way to see his play *Chicken Soup with Barley*. This was the first part of Arnold's autobiographical trilogy and dealt with his youth in the East End of London. I was delighted by it, so much so that after the performance I went backstage hoping to find the author. There I met a short, slightly stocky and very Jewish-looking young man. He had a faint East End accent and wore a signet ring. I told him I was a publisher and he was clearly pleased that I had taken the trouble to come so far to see his play.

Back in London we quickly became friends. Arnold invited me to his home and there I met Dusty, his wife-to-be. Arnold loved to talk about his work, about the theatre, and I liked to listen. I was invited again and again. Sometimes it was just family, at other times it was a mixed group of writers, critics and actors. A regular group. On occasions there was a large gathering. Arnold adored entertaining and Dusty loved to cook, and so when a foreign theatre company, usually one who had performed Arnold's work, came to London, he would invite the entire company to dinner, even when there were twenty or thirty of them. At the time I lived alone in my house in Chalcot Crescent, and greatly enjoyed the evenings out with what had become my surrogate family.

At Penguin I published *Chicken Soup with Barley* in the first volume of the series *New English Dramatists* that I launched there. At that time the Royal Court Theatre committed to putting on Arnold's trilogy. This meant *Chicken Soup* immediately followed by *Roots* (which incidentally had Joan Plowright in the lead, giving a superb performance) and then *I'm Talking about Jerusalem*. Later, at Cape, I published all three plays and we called the book *The Wesker Trilogy*. It was not long before my friend was recognized as one of the most important playwrights of the time along with John Osborne and Harold Pinter. Of course Arnold was delighted by his success but it did not seem to go to his head.

The Royal Court Theatre became something of a second home to me. My prime interest was in Arnold and the other playwrights, but I also got to know the management, especially George Devine, the head of the theatre, and Tony Richardson, his deputy and an exceptionally talented director of stage and film. George commissioned me to write a Christmas pantomime based on *Jack and the Beanstalk*. Then he invited me to attend a photocall for Lord Snowdon (Tony Armstrong-Jones as he then was) to take a photograph of all those connected with the Royal Court. We were on an open bus which was parked outside the theatre. I was very proud to be a part of this scene. The photograph itself has been reproduced various times, firstly in *Vogue* and then in John Osborne's autobiography.

At the Court I became friends with some of the actors and in particular with Robert Shaw. He was an exceptionally intelligent man and I was greatly impressed by his first novel, *The Hiding Place*. I frequently went with him to his home in St John's Wood where we would play table tennis for hours on end. It was a fast and tough game. I thought I was good but he was better. Much better. He was also fanatically competitive. Another little game he would play at a party was to hang from a veranda and challenge others to hang for as long as he could.

Bob's wife was a white Jamaican and they had several daughters. He came to play the lead in a Restoration play at the Royal Court opposite Mary Ure and they had an affair. Mary became pregnant and she and Bob's wife were due to give birth at around the same time. This led Bob to make a horrendous declaration. He told his wife and Mary that he would choose between them according to whichever bore him a son. It turned out to be Mary and thereupon he left his wife. At this time he was a celebrated actor and later he became a famous film star.

Arnold had the idea for Centre 42, which was named after Resolution 42 passed by the Trade Union Congress in 1960. The object was to bring the arts to the nation, i.e. to take them out of London. The Centre needed headquarters and Arnold focused upon the Round House in Chalk Farm as the ideal building. The Centre had no funds, and although Arnold was beginning to earn well, it certainly wasn't well enough for him to finance such an organization, otherwise I have no doubt he would have done so. He turned Centre 42 into a charity and determined to persuade Louis Mintz, the owner of the Round House, to donate his lease of the building. I well remember Arnold's triumph the day he succeeded. Meanwhile, as a display of democracy, he decided to appoint a board for Centre 42 including Michael Croft, Sean Kenny, Jenny Lee, John McGrath and Alun Owen. He also asked me to join, and I did.

We met monthly. After two or three meetings I came to realize the degree to which Arnold was autocratic. Much as I valued our friendship, I found myself more frequently in opposition than in agreement with him. I arranged to meet with Arnold and gave him two alternatives: either I would resign or I would feel obliged to oppose him when I was so minded. With all the charm in the world he said, 'Well, then it would be best if you resign.'

I did not feel equipped to reciprocate Arnold and Dusty's hospitality in London but from time to time I invited them to my cottage in the Black Mountains, a place for which they came to share my passion. And then, one day, when I was striding across the mountains, I came upon a semi-ruined cottage in a marvellous position. The house was wildly neglected and I had a hunch it might be for sale. Without losing any time I made enquiries and tracked down the owner. He told me that the cottage was indeed for sale but it was 'under offer', for £2,000. I was so disappointed that I asked him whether he might be tempted by a higher offer. With the characteristic shrewdness of a Welsh farmer, he answered that this would depend entirely on the sum in question. I found a telephone booth just outside Hay-on-Wye, rang Arnold in London and was thrilled to find him at home. I said he should come down the following day. This proved impossible, but he and Dusty came the day after. It was love at first sight, as I knew it would be. I suggested that if they really wanted the house the obvious offer was £2,500. No less, and no need for more. Arnold said they could not afford it, and so I offered to lend them the money. I also pointed out the obvious fact that they could just sit on the house until they had the money to do it up. I guessed that the repairs would cost in the region of £7,000–£10,000 and in such a context the extra £500 surely wouldn't matter. Arnold agreed. We made the offer and I insisted on an immediate response. The offer was accepted, and so Arnold and Dusty became my neighbours in Wales.

By now Arnold was not just a very close friend, he was my 'best friend', and as best friends do, we confided in each other. He told me that in addition to his three children I knew in London (one of whom was my god-daughter), he had a daughter in Sweden, conceived while he was in Stockholm with one of his plays. He had not learnt about the child until after it was born. At that point, I was the only person in the world he'd told and of course it had to remain a secret, which it did for a further fifteen years.

For a good number of years Cape continued to publish Arnold's plays, even when they were not performed in England. Unsurprisingly we sold very few copies. One day – I do not recall how many books we had published and how much money we had lost by then – I said to Arnold, 'Look, I think we should wait until your new play is performed before we publish it here.' Arnold regarded this not simply as disloyalty but as treachery. It seems hard to believe, but his anger was so great that he did not speak to me for twenty-five years. I would not have thought that such a thing could happen to an intimate friendship.

And then, about a year ago, I was alone in my cottage in the Black Mountains, when I caught a debilitating ear infection. I urgently needed a doctor, if not a hospital, but I could not possibly drive. My wife Regina rang Arnold at his house in Wales and he immediately phoned a doctor. Arnold came to fetch me and although we hardly spoke in the car there was a tenderness between us. Inspired by this chance meeting after so very many years, I invited Arnold to dinner when I returned to the cottage a few weeks later. He accepted graciously and we talked for hours. Almost like old times. Of course, I thought of attempting to discuss what had happened between us, but I did not wish to risk damaging the evening. And nor did he.

THE TRIUMVIRATE

I HAVE CALLED this section 'The Triumvirate' because it is
about three writers, all English. They came into my life at
approximately the same time and they were especially talented.
I am speaking of Ian McEwan, Martin Amis and Julian Barnes.
They were much the same age when they joined Cape and in
each case we have published them from the very beginning
of their careers. Now, many years later, they are still Cape
authors. Such loyalty is uncommon in publishing these days.
They also happened to be the best of friends, with one important hiccup which we will come to later. They loved to compete,
especially at tennis and snooker, though rather less so when it
came to the Booker Prize. But, of course, they were obliged to
do so. The fact is that these three writers were not simply stars
on the Cape list, they were all three deemed, almost from the
beginning, to be among the very best 'young British writers'.
I published, in addition, a fourth writer of comparable talent
and of a similar age. I have not written about him here because
he was not part of the same 'gang', but have devoted the
following section to him. I am speaking of Bruce Chatwin,
who died in 1989.

MARTIN AMIS

I met Martin Amis at Lemmons, in Barnet, the country house belonging to his father and Kingsley's wife Elizabeth Jane Howard, a Cape author from before my time. Martin was at Oxford at the time, and it was Jane (as opposed to Kingsley) who was responsible for encouraging him to go to university. Martin was a precocious boy of eighteen and, although he expressed no particular interest in writing a novel, I had a hunch that he would, and encouraged him to send the book to me if and when he wrote one. Several years after we had first met I was surprised to receive *The Rachel Papers*. I say surprised because if I had been him I would have gone out of my way to avoid my father's publisher and to find my own. Martin became the first of the Triumvirate to be published by Cape.

We met frequently for weekends at Lemmons. Martin came alone and I came with a variety of girlfriends. We always greeted each other with a kiss on both cheeks – with my French background this comes quite naturally to me but I was surprised that Martin adopted the habit so readily. I recall his telling me some years later that he was greatly impressed by my selection of girlfriends. But it was not very long before he began to follow suit. The very first time I took Martin out to dinner he asked if he could bring a friend. The friend turned out to be Tina Brown, also at Oxford; she was not just a pretty girl, she had some success as a playwright very early on. Later she became a superstar journalist and editor of *Vanity Fair* in England and America, and was then appointed editor of the *New Yorker*. While in England she married Harold Evans, the fabled editor of the *Sunday Times*. Meanwhile Martin moved on to Gully Wells, stepdaughter of A. J. Ayer, then Claire Tomalin, widow of Nick and now partner of Michael

Frayn, and others besides, many of them well known in the literary world.

Martin's career as a novelist progressed quickly. His first novel, *The Rachel Papers*, was relatively conventional, and then he developed a style of his own which was as powerful as it was different from that of other writers. I am puzzled by the fact that in the Booker stakes Martin should have done the least well of our Triumvirate: certainly this does not make him a lesser writer than the others. He began to acquire a real and considerable following of his own. As a companion (not that I saw a great deal of him) he was stimulating and witty. But he had a weak side. I am thinking of the way in which he handled his desire to join the American literary agency of Andrew Wylie, aka 'the jackal'. This move was not in itself reprehensible, but Martin forgot to tell his agent, Pat Kavanagh, who, to make matters worse, happened to be the wife of his best friend, Julian Barnes. This resulted in a sizzling letter from Julian, declaring that he would never forgive Martin and there could be no question of any future contact between them.

Martin is deeply serious about his work, so much so that it is only with great reluctance he will accept an invitation to lunch since, as he puts it, lunch 'cuts into' his day. I am under the impression he is highly deliberate in his life which makes the following incident all the more inexplicable. We had arranged (with his approval of course) and advertised and promoted a signing for his new novel at the Covent Garden Bookshop. The day before the signing – literally the day before – Martin rang to say he would not be able to attend. 'What do you mean?' asked our Promotions Director. 'I'm getting married tomorrow,' said Martin.

IAN McEWAN

Ian McEwan was the second of the Triumvirate I took on. In those days my eagerness to find new writers was such that I made time to read numerous literary magazines. In two of these, *The American Literary Review* (edited by Ted Solotaroff) and the *New English Review* (edited by Ian Hamilton), I came across stories by a young writer called McEwan. I found the stories most striking. They were bizarre, macabre and sometimes very funny. I wrote to the author saying that if he had enough stories to make a book, I would be most interested in publishing it. He wrote back saying, 'Sorry, but my book is committed to another publisher' (Tom Rosenthal at Secker & Warburg), and that seemed to be that. However, I continued my magazine reading and over the months came across further McEwan stories. They seemed to be getting even better. After a year of this, I wrote to him again saying that I had not seen any announcement of the publication of his stories and asking what was happening. He replied that Rosenthal had told him that on second thoughts it would be best to publish a novel first and then follow with the stories. Ian had dutifully accepted this proposal but found himself unable to write to the length of a novel. I replied offering a contract for the stories forthwith and unconditionally, and so we came to publish *First Love, Last Rites*.

When we signed the contract I told Ian that I would be happy to publish a second volume of stories if that was his preference. Whilst *First Love*, as we called it, did not take off immediately, it went on to sell hundreds of thousands of copies, a phenomenal number for any book and almost unheard of for a book of stories. In the event we followed *First Love* with a second book of stories: *In Between the Sheets*. Since then Ian has written nine novels. The most admired and the most successful was *Atonement* (2001), although he won the Booker Prize with *Amsterdam* (1998). Of the Triumvirate only he has won the prize.

Some writers take being on the shortlist for the Booker philosophically, whatever the outcome. Ian is not one of these, although normally he seems calm and considered. When he was shortlisted for *Black Dogs*, his expectations were high. I shall always remember the moment when the name of the winner was announced. Ian turned to me at our dinner table and said, 'Let's get out of here,' and so all twelve of us seated at the Cape table left together and we had a party at my apartment. This was even before the speeches. I watched the proceedings on video the following evening. In the Guildhall, filled with almost the entire literary world dressed up in their dinner jackets, there stood one lonely empty table.

Regina and I have seen a good deal of Ian over the years and have come to admire him both as a person and as a father. He adores his two sons, now teenagers, and frequently takes them alone on independent adventures. His wife Penny, from whom he is now divorced, sometimes complained (with justification) that she felt left out because my principal interest was so obviously in Ian. And so Regina and I decided to make a special effort and invited the McEwans, just the two of them, to dinner at our Eaton Place flat. At that time they lived in Oxford. The dinner invitation was for eight o'clock. At ten past nine a somewhat dishevelled Ian arrived at our front door. 'Where's Penny?' I asked. 'We had a row and she jumped out of the car at a traffic light,' came the reply. This seemed ironical, for it occurred just as we were determined to make an effort on her behalf. Ian is now happily married to Annalena McAfee.

JULIAN BARNES

My three authors are completely dissimilar in their personalities. If Martin is the fast-talking one and also the best-looking, then Julian Barnes (who was the third to be published by us) is the strong, silent one, with Ian McEwan somewhere in between. Speaking of silent, I recall taking Julian to lunch at a smart and not particularly noisy restaurant. For several minutes we sat gazing at each other without exchanging a word and then Julian said, 'Tom, I asked you a question. Did you not hear it?' Nowadays I have a hearing aid and I hope that this kind of thing will not reoccur.

Julian came to us with *Metroland*, his first novel. It was a book I liked but no more than that. Then, however, came *Flaubert's Parrot* (1984), for which I have a real passion. This novel is both highly original and extremely entertaining. It has given enormous pleasure to many thousands of readers, regardless of whether they have read Flaubert or not. In England *Flaubert's Parrot* received some superb reviews, was shortlisted for the Booker Prize and sold well. In France it caused a sensation, helped on its way by Bernard Pivot, the leading French literary TV pundit and a man with an enormous following. While interviewing Julian at the time of *Flaubert's Parrot*, Pivot said to camera, 'Go out and buy this book.' His viewers did.

When Julian and his wife Pat Kavanagh came down to visit us in the South of France we took them to Apt, our local market town. There is a bookshop on the main square and as we entered the owner immediately greeted Julian with, 'Welcome, Monsieur Barnes.' This was a year or two after the television interview. Julian speaks superb French and loves all things French, be it literature, food or wine. He also has style. Within an hour of arriving at our house he said, 'Could I look at your *Gault Millau*? I want to take you and Regina out to the best restaurant in the region,' and so he did.

At the time of my sixtieth birthday Julian gave a dinner party for me at his home. He cooked a memorable meal, the more so for the fact that between the main course and the dessert we suddenly noticed that Julian had disappeared. Pat went to look for him and returned announcing that he was lying on his bed fast asleep! Clearly the dinner which was as elaborate as it was wonderful had taken its toll.

After *Parrot*, as we call it, came *A History of the World in 10½ Chapters*. It is as imaginative as the title would indicate, and although it has nothing in common with *Parrot*, it is a book I like as much. These two books are equally masterly. A verbal example of Julian's wit came about when Liz Calder left Cape to co-found Bloomsbury. He was asked whether he intended to follow her. He replied, 'Why would I want to go with her when it is she who has left me?'

BRUCE CHATWIN

BRUCE CHATWIN was of the same generation as the Triumvirate but I will treat him separately because, alas, he is dead. His talent was certainly comparable with that of Martin Amis, Ian McEwan and Julian Barnes.

I was introduced to Bruce's work by an article he had written about nomads, sent to me by his agent Deborah Rogers. With her usual perspicacity she thought she had discovered a new and special writer. In my experience of all the literary agents in England, Deborah is the most likely to be right when it comes to quality. I was impressed by the article and, even on so little evidence, I was happy to offer a contract. However, when Bruce sent me the first eighty pages of the book I found them stilted, even boring. He came to my office and I knew it would be a particularly difficult meeting. Obviously I had to be frank and equally obviously he was exceedingly disappointed. Despite my misgivings about what I had read, I had absolutely no regrets about the contract we offered. I feared that I might have lost Bruce but this was not the way it turned out. It was as though what he had written was an aberration and would bear no relation to whatever might be forthcoming.

Prior to becoming a writer, Bruce worked at Sotheby's, initially in a most humble capacity when he was only eighteen, becoming, at the age of twenty-three, their specialist in Impres-

Amusing myself
in the garden at
Crazies Hill

In between
bouts of
washing up
on the *Kedmah*
en route
for Israel

'Working' on the set of the film studio in Munich

Reading at home in Chalcot Crescent

At work in Venice

Together with Graham C. Greene at 30 Bedford Square

The publication-day party for *Declaration*. From left to right, Bill Hopkins, John Wain, Lindsay Andersen, me, Doris Lessing, and Kenneth Tynan

A seminar on the
Wesker Trilogy.
On the left,
Arnold Wesker
and on the right,
Frederic Raphael

Setting off on the
Aldermaston march.
Left to right: Elaine
Dundy (married to
Kenneth Tynan),
me, Kenneth Tynan

Doris Lessing in my
Bedford Square office

Mr & Mrs Arthur
Rubinstein, celebrating
our publication of
his autobiography

At Carney with, left to right, Tom Wiseman, John Fowles, Frederic Raphael

Arnold and Dusty Wesker – breakfast at Carney

My mother, Rita

My father

Presenting an Emil to Babette Cole, winner of the Kurt Maschler Prize

Sidney Bernstein with my son Ben

Joseph Heller, Regina,
and Jo's wife Valerie

William Styron

Philip Roth and
Claire Bloom

John Irving

Karel Reisz, Betsy Blair and Regina at La Masure

Roald Dahl with Hannah, Alice and Ben

Bob Gottlieb playing
table tennis at Carney

With Gabriel García Márquez

Allen Ginsberg astride an American plane shot down by the Cubans
near Havana

Two Cape authors:
Roberto Calasso and
Salman Rushdie

On the eve of
the Booker Prize
I brought in
a 65 kilo tuna

Judging *The Times* collection of detective stories, from left to right, R. A. Butler, John Higgins (of *The Times*), Tom Stoppard, me and Agatha Christie

sionist and modern art. He had a magnificent eye and could have had an outstanding career in the art world. But, even so early on, he grew restless and began to dislike the world of the auction house. He decided to retire from it. It was a brave decision, especially as he had virtually no money.

After the nomads episode Bruce made no comment to me about his future writing plans. He had taken a job at the *Sunday Times* writing articles on a variety of subjects. This also was to be shortlived. Without warning, he left and sent a telegram to the newspaper saying simply, 'Gone to Patagonia'.

Some three years later I received a completed manuscript from Bruce. It was entitled *In Patagonia*. He had written a travel book like no other I had ever read. It was an account of his discoveries in this remote part of Argentina. The text was fragmentary yet compelling. I was ecstatic about the book, about the form, the style and the content. It seemed like a miracle after the false start on nomads and is, to date, one of my favourite books. I think it is probably also the Chatwin book I like best of all, and, for once, a book I especially admired got some decent reviews.

At this time I was able to get to know Bruce a bit. I say a bit, because he was always elusive and always secretive about his whereabouts and his friendships. Physically Bruce was strikingly attractive. In conversation he was scintillating. He was such a good raconteur that it was difficult to believe he could also be a good writer. The two rarely go together.

Later, while Bruce was writing *On the Black Hill*, the story of a pair of twins who lived their entire lives in the Black Mountains, a remote area which even today is much as it was a hundred years ago, I lent him my stone cottage in Wales. It is on the mountain, just near Capel-Y-Ffin (Chapel at the End). Bruce stayed for five months and I know that various people visited him there but I could not name a single one of them. Bruce was a great walker and in between bouts of writing he

strode across the hills. While in Wales he met the singer George
Melly and, on occasions, Penelope Betjeman, wife of the poet
John Betjeman. I learned of these encounters from mutual
friends – Bruce never mentioned them. I also learned from
Nicholas Shakespeare's biography that Bruce had been to
Capel-Y-Ffin as a young boy. Even this is something he chose
not to tell me. Considering that my cottage was an important
part of my life and that I had lent it to him, this strikes me as
strange.

After *On the Black Hill* came the book many consider to
be Bruce's masterpiece, *Songlines*. Again a great deal of travel
was involved, this time in Australia. The title is derived from
the songlines of the Aborigines. Bruce's fascination with primitive peoples made *Songlines* especially close to his heart, though
each new book became a passionate love affair for him.

I do not know when Bruce contracted his mysterious
disease but he was certainly very ill at the time we were putting
together his book *What Am I Doing Here*. He came to my
office for a picnic lunch and we had to help him on to the
couch. He had given me a transparency to use for the jacket.
It was like an abstract painting. I asked Bruce who took the
photograph and he said, 'I did.' Shortly afterwards I went with
Regina to visit Bruce at his home, Homer End. He was even
more frail. Elizabeth, his wife, had made up a day-bed for him.
She was a constant anchor in his life. Wherever he travelled,
and with whomsoever he travelled, he always returned to her.

From his day-bed, in a soft, spellbinding voice, he spoke of
the novel he would write next. The heroine, I recall, was called
Lydia Livingston and the setting was Moscow, Paris and New
York. Such a wide range represented a new departure for Bruce
and I think the book would have been his most important. But
we knew that he would not have time to write it.

Bruce died in 1989. Theories of the cause of his death vary.
Some said it was AIDS, which would make sense, given his

relationships. Others said it was a Chinese fungus he had contracted two or three years previously. It may even have been both. His memorial service was held at the Russian Orthodox Church in London. It was the day after the *fatwa* against Salman Rushdie had been declared. None the less, Salman was present, slipping out just before the end. I was looking particularly tanned and a journalist asked me if I was Salman. I said, 'No, he's over there,' pointing at Harold Pinter.

Approximately a year after Bruce's death Elizabeth came to see me, carrying a large plastic bag crammed full of 35mm negatives which he had taken. She wondered whether they might be of any interest. They certainly were. They were wonderful and I decided to invite David King to design the book. I spent many happy hours with this brilliant man, making a selection for what became a beautiful picture book. The extraordinary thing was that neither David King nor any of Bruce's closest friends knew that he took photographs.

We launched our book with a show at the Hayward Gallery. It was a jolly gathering of Bruce's friends. I had a squabble with one of them, George Melly, who overheard me telling someone that Bruce had written *On a Black Hill* in my cottage. He interrupted with, 'What absolute nonsense, Bruce wrote the book at our house.' He was really agitated but I refused to give in and suggested we share the honour and say Bruce wrote the book in both our houses.

SALMAN RUSHDIE

SALMAN CAME TO US when Liz Calder joined Cape, which coincided with his having finished his draft of *Midnight's Children*. Many think of this as being his first novel but it was not. That was *Grimus*. I found reading *Midnight's Children* a marvellous experience. The novel belongs firmly to the literature that has been called 'magic realism'. It is a magnificent example of it. Although Salman was clearly Liz's author, I loved the book with such a passion that she was happy for me to share in the publishing process. Almost everyone at Cape was equally enthusiastic, and we were convinced that it would become a bestseller, but at the time of publication we had sold a mere 2,000 copies. Then the novel won the Booker Prize. It was not long before sales reached 40,000, then 50,000 and then 60,000. The excitement upon the announcement at the Booker Prize dinner was without parallel in my experience of the prize.

A Booker dinner years later was a very different matter. I was again seated by Salman. He had written another superb book, *Shame*, which some considered superior to *Midnight's Children*. Shortly after the winner had been announced (it was Coetze), Fay Weldon, the Chairperson of the judges, came up to our table. Believe it or not, she said to Salman, 'I just want you to know that *Shame* was definitely the best book. But the best book does not always win.' Salman was furious. Rightly so.

There is a third Rushdie Booker experience to be mentioned. It was in 1995 and on this occasion Salman and I were separated by 2,000 miles. His book *The Moor's Last Sigh* was on the shortlist. In my capacity as the 'founder' of the Booker Prize I have been invited to the dinner every year and I have attended them all. Except this one. The reason was that I was sailing in the Indonesian ocean. On the night of the Booker, we had just left Irian Jaya where we had visited a head-hunting tribe, most of whom had never seen a white man. There were eighteen passengers aboard our boat. A number of them were Indonesian, including a man called Amir, and none was the least bit famous except for one couple: Mick Jagger and Jerry Hall. They had booked two cabins, one for themselves and one for Jerry's clothes. Just as the Booker dinner was taking place in London, I was out at sea in a dinghy with two of the other passengers. I had of course told everyone about the Booker and my hopes for Salman. While I was absent from the main ship, Amir heard on the radio that Salman had won the prize. He told Regina and she rushed out in another dinghy to come and tell me the good news. Now, I am a hopeless fisherman, but as luck would have it I had just hooked an enormous tuna. When we landed the fish we found it weighed 130lb. The process of bringing it in took well over an hour. Regina found me totally engrossed with the excitement of my fish.

Back at the boat I changed for dinner and ordered champagne for everyone. It went perfectly with the tuna sushi we enjoyed that night. Before dinner I wrote a fax of congratulations to send to Salman. Mick Jagger asked if he could add something. It emerged that he had met Salman on a few occasions and had read several of his books. Try as we might, the fax would not go through. It wasn't until we got back to Bali several days later that I discovered Salman had not won the Booker after all. Amir must have heard his name and assumed that they were announcing the winner. I was greatly relieved my fax had failed to reach Salman.

The Satanic Verses was submitted to us by Andrew Wylie, Salman's new agent. A combination of the fact that Wylie was asking for £500,000 and that neither I nor my colleagues were hugely enthusiastic about the book resulted in our declining. Penguin were eager to acquire Salman, whatever the advance, and so they did, but, as everyone knows, it was this book that led to the *fatwa*. Publishing it turned into a nightmare for Penguin. *The Satanic Verses* became a full-time preoccupation for Peter Mayer, the Penguin Chief Executive: Salman's life was constantly under threat and even the Penguin staff felt endangered. The Norwegian publisher of the book was shot three times and left for dead outside his home and the Japanese translator was stabbed to death. For several years Salman was obliged to move from safe house to safe house at regular intervals.

I never had any idea where Salman was living, but I was in possession of a telephone number which always reached him without problem. It was several months after the *fatwa* was declared that Regina and I invited Salman to dinner. On the morning of the dinner, the police came to our apartment to check the place out. Then, in the evening, Salman arrived accompanied by four policemen. None of them intruded on the dinner. Two stayed upstairs in a spare room watching television and two waited in a police car outside the house.

Salman's minders always came along when he visited our offices. Sometimes I would see two men wearing suits and ties in our canteen which would signal to me that Salman was somewhere in the building. So much for security! I once asked Salman who paid for his protection. Although he did not wish to be specific, he said that the government paid the largest part but he personally contributed a good deal.

We thought it would be restful for Salman to come and

stay with us in France. Our house is comfortable and it is in a remote spot. He got excited at the prospect and negotiated with the French government for months. But, as he had told us from the beginning, he would only come if his presence were not to result in our house being surrounded by French police. It seemed impossible to avoid this. The issue went as far as discussions with President Mitterrand but in the end French bureaucracy defeated Salman.

In the midst of his difficulties the National Portrait Gallery commissioned a painting of Salman. His friend, the poet James Fenton, gave a little party to celebrate. It was a buffet and one of the dishes was chicken tikka. I was talking to Salman, animated and gesticulating as usual. At the same time I was chewing some chicken tikka. And then I was coughing and choking. I went to the lavatory to try to bring up the bone that was stuck in my throat. I had no success and lay down on a couch, finding it increasingly difficult to breathe. Salman was wonderfully solicitous and quick to realize that I was in serious trouble, and took matters into his own hands. He rang for an ambulance and Regina and I were driven off to an emergency ward. The hospital x-rayed my throat and announced that they could not find anything stuck there. At home, I got through the night with difficulty, but the following morning I was eager to go to the office. Regina insisted that we go instead to Harley Street. There I was operated upon immediately and they removed the bone the hospital had failed to find.

RETURN TO AMERICA

JOSEPH HELLER notwithstanding, the American first novel it has given me the greatest satisfaction to publish was by Tom Pynchon. I was introduced to his work approximately a year after *Catch-22*. The source was the same, i.e. my favourite American literary agent, Candida Donadio. 'I have something for you,' she told me enigmatically. The following day a very large package was hand-delivered to the Blackstone Hotel in New York, where I was staying. The manuscript was called *V* and it was by an unknown writer called Tom Pynchon. Not only was he unknown as a writer, he was also unknown as a man. He made a point of avoiding any literary circle. He has even managed from 1961 to date to avoid being photographed.

Reading *V* was an exceptional experience, quite unlike any other. The writing had an almost psychedelic quality. I felt as though I was reading a literary mystery story. And all this was, for me, heightened by a heavy and constant snowfall just outside my window. I continued to read all weekend as the snow continued to fall. A great deal of territory is covered in the book and when, many years later, I finally got to meet Pynchon and complimented him on the fact that he had portrayed numerous countries so accurately, he told me to my amazement that with the exception of Valletta, in Malta, he had never been to a single one of the places he depicted.

It was maddening not to be able to meet, nor even correspond with, a writer one so greatly admired. I pleaded with Candida, as she obviously knew Pynchon's whereabouts, but to no avail. She said he did not want her to tell anyone where he was and that was that. My only consolation, if a consolation it can be called, was that at the same time his American publisher (Viking) had not met him either. *V* was a triumph in the States. In England the reviews were mixed and although some adored the book, it has to this day remained underrated. We went on to publish Pynchon's *The Crying of Lot 49*, and then an extremely difficult book, which many considered to be his masterpiece, *Gravity's Rainbow*. This won the National Book Award in America. Characteristically, Pynchon did not turn up for the ceremony.

One day – it must have been some fifteen years after our publication of *V* – Patsy, our telephonist at Bedford Square, rang me to say that someone called Tom Pynchon was asking for me on the phone. I suspect she instinctively knew this was a special event. I said, 'Are you sure of the name?' and then, 'Please put him through.' I was in a hurry lest he cut off.

My first words were, 'Where are you?' and he said he was at the British Museum. 'That's just around the corner,' I replied.

'I know,' he said. The British Museum was a five-minute walk from my office.

'When can we meet?' I asked.

'What about now?' he suggested. What had been so difficult for so many years had suddenly become so very simple. It is hard to describe my excitement as I waited.

The five minutes seemed to take an eternity and then a tall, lanky figure, good-looking in an eccentric way, was ushered into my office. He was very much at ease and I felt as though we had known each other for years. My first question was to ask what had brought him to London. Tom told me he was writing a novel based on the lives of two British engineers called Mason and Dixon and that much of the research material was to be found in the British Museum. These two men had gone on to work in America and the Mason–Dixon Line was named after them. There was so much to say but I had another appointment and so, extremely diffidently, in the light of Tom's famous need for secrecy, I explained that my then wife Fay was the leading London restaurant critic, which made spontaneous dinner invitations easy to arrange. I asked whether he might like to join us for dinner in a restaurant that evening. Tom said that he would love to and took down the address. It was so easy and I could not resist asking him why he had been so elusive for so many years. It was a question he politely ignored.

Tom turned up on the dot at the appointed venue. During dinner I asked him if he would be free to join us the following night and, again, he was delighted to accept. None of this remotely tied in with the recluse image. Then two days later I ventured to ask whether he might like to have dinner at our home and if so would it be all right if we were to invite a few, just a very few, friends? Tom had no problem with that either. We rang some friends, choosing ardent Pynchon fans of course. They found it difficult to believe that they were on the verge of meeting the man himself. The evening was a triumph except for one moment early on when I asked Tom to inscribe a copy of *V* and he declined. 'I'm sorry,' he said. After dinner I tried again, and I am happy to say that I am now the proud owner of a copy of *V* signed by the author.

We saw each other every other day for two weeks and then one day I rang Tom at the flat he had rented (characteristically,

For Tom Maschler —
CHEERS!
Thomas Pinchon

he had declined to give me the address) and found that the telephone had been cut off. I was disappointed he had not said goodbye, but I knew the need to move on must have been urgent. I subsequently discovered that an editor at the American publishing house Random House had sent Tom a proof copy of a novel called *Faggots* by Larry Kramer. The book was for some extraordinary reason intercepted by the police who appeared to find it obscene. In his paranoia, Tom fled lest the police seek him out, despite the fact that he had no connection whatsoever to the book, nor was in any way responsible for the fact that it had been sent it to him.

When the manuscript of Tom's new novel, *Vineland*, was ready for submission, he issued instructions that it must not be offered to us at Jonathan Cape. This was because he had read in the *New York Times* that Si Newhouse, the owner of Random House, had recently bought Jonathan Cape. It was a sad blow. By this time Tom had married his American agent, Melanie Jackson, and I rang and pleaded with her but to no avail. Tom was determined that the remotest connection with Random House be avoided at all costs.

On a subsequent visit to New York I received a phone call from Melanie saying that Tom would very much like it if I could have a drink with him. We made a date and Tom turned up at the Pierre Hotel, where I was staying at the time. He was carrying a plastic bag and in it was a copy of *Vineland*. Not only a copy of *Vineland* but an inscribed copy! I was profoundly touched. After that we did come to publish *Mason and Dixon* and I trust we shall publish Tom's next book. But he is a slow writer. In the interim Regina and I invariably have lunch or dinner with Tom and Melanie on our New York visits. They have produced a boy whom Tom calls 'the kid'. When we had lunch in New York shortly after 'the kid' was born, Tom produced two cigars, one for me to smoke and one for him to smoke to celebrate the birth (a classic Pynchon gesture).

Beyond Joseph Heller and Tom Pynchon, Candida was the source of a good number of other writers I came to publish. One who has remained especially vivid in my mind is Bruce Jay Friedman. Again, it was a first novel. The book was called *A Mother's Kisses*. Like its author, it was extremely funny and very Jewish and had a considerable success in America but not in England. Via Bruce a totally new and different weekend experience was in store for me: Fire Island. This is located an hour or so by car from New York. Then you arrive at a ferry and thereafter it is a twenty-minute ride. The island has a magnificent long white sandy beach and I was amazed by its proximity to New York.

From my reading of American novels I supposed that Fire Island was 100 per cent homosexual, but I discovered there were also a couple of heterosexual communities and Bruce's house was in one of them. Fire Island was not a place where *some* smoke pot – there were only a very few who did not.

And everyone drinks heavily. On the Saturday of my weekend Bruce gave a party. At around midnight I was exhausted by the noise level. The party showed signs of continuing all night and so I asked where I might sleep. This was clearly something no one had thought about. Bruce showed me to a bedroom and I finally managed to fall asleep. In the middle of the night I was woken by a woman who burst into my room closely pursued by a man. She took off her clothes and got into my bed. The man did likewise and they began to fuck. That is the only word for it. They finished quickly and left as suddenly as they had arrived.

*

ON MY THIRD TRIP to New York I bought the publishing rights in a book of essays called *Candy Stream Line Flake Baby*. The author was a leading exponent of the 'new journalism'. His name was Tom Wolfe. In addition to being an excellent essayist and a superb stylist with a range from art to astronauts, he was something of a celebrity about town and a famous ladies' man. A trademark of Tom's, then and now, has been the wearing of white suits. I remember our Publicity Director asking him when he was in London how he managed to keep his suit so immaculately white. He took her to his dressing room and opened the cupboard. There, hanging in a row, were six perfect white suits.

To this day, Tom tells the story of my meeting him at Heathrow on his first trip to London. To celebrate his arrival (in a white suit of course) I could not resist meeting him on my Vespa. I had of course also hired a taxi to transport his numerous pieces of luggage. At first the prospect of that Vespa ride clearly made Tom extremely nervous and I could see that he was thinking of declining. But he did not utter a word and by the time we arrived at his favourite hotel, the Connaught, I felt he was getting into the spirit of the thing.

Tom went on to write several works of non-fiction and then he decided to embark on a novel. He would require several years to write it and so he very reasonably expected a substantial advance. My confidence in his writing talent, as in his intelligence, was such that I was perfectly ready to put up a great deal of money. I think this is the first and only time I have ever commissioned a first novel for an extremely large sum. The writing procedure Tom chose was for the first draft to be serialized in *Rolling Stone* and then for him to rewrite the book for hardcover publication. The novel was called *The Bonfire of the Vanities*. It is inordinately well constructed and extremely readable. In no way does the book show the mark of a beginner. It was a triumphant success both sides of the Atlantic. Even now, many years later, Tom continues to express his gratitude for the confidence we showed.

I have said little as yet of the man. He is exceptionally gracious, soft-spoken and well-read, and has immaculate manners. He is also outstandingly intelligent, with the enquiring mind of a superb journalist. He is a passionately caring person. Many years ago Regina had a mysterious ailment that we thought the Mayo Clinic in America might cure. Tom went out of his way to introduce us to not one but two of the leading professors there and he wrote to them as if we were his closest friends.

Recently Regina and I took Tom and Sheila to a particularly smart restaurant in New York and I chose one of my favourite wines, a Vosne Romanée. We were enjoying ourselves: the hors d'œuvre had just been cleared away and we were looking forward to the main course. Just then the lady at the next table made a slightly exaggerated gesture and knocked over our bottle of red wine. Tom's suit, which had of course been white as ever, was horribly stained by the red wine. The lady was abject with apologies; numerous waiters rushed over in a forlorn effort to repair the damage. Tom was gracious as ever but I could feel that he was gritting his teeth and from then on all conversation became strained. Each of us made an effort and yet the evening was ruined.

*

I AM PROUD to say that many of my American authors have become good friends. The fact that we see one another only once a year does not apparently stand in the way of this. Of all the American writers there is one who has become a particularly staunch friend and that is Kurt Vonnegut. As most readers will know, Kurt began his career as a science fiction writer, initially writing what is frequently (and unflatteringly) called 'pulp fiction'. Then came *Cat's Cradle*, which was hailed as 'quality science fiction'. Thereafter Kurt began to 'go straight' and this is when we became his publisher.

When I first met Kurt, he was living in Cape Cod. He had invited me to stay for the weekend and I was fortunate to have hit upon a special annual event which Kurt had invented. Before describing the procedure he assured me that if I did not like the sound of it I must feel under no obligation to participate. Of course I could not resist joining in. This is what it was about. Near Kurt's house (it was really more of a barn) a mud lake had formed. It was wet and squidgy all year round and some three or four feet deep. The game was for all participants, Kurt of course included (and he had the advantage of being exceptionally tall), to line up along one side of the lake. They took off simultaneously and made for the opposite side. The lake was about 100 metres wide, a tiny distance, but the going was rough and the journey took as much as an hour. Competitors emerged covered from head to toe in thick mud. Kurt was invariably one of the first, and sat on the bank chortling with delight.

As it turned out, my visit also coincided with the end of Kurt's marriage. In classic Vonnegut fashion he and his first wife have remained the best of friends. I think she subsequently married a judge and Kurt, for whatever reason, finds this a hoot. Meanwhile, he took up with an attractive but tough photographer named Jill Kremetz. Perhaps 'pushy' would describe her more accurately than 'tough'. This lady is something of a legend in New York literary circles and everyone who has had dealings with her can relate a Jill Kremetz story or two. The stories I tell will come as no surprise to anyone who knows Jill, and no one knows her better than her husband. They are as true of Jill as is the fact that Kurt loves her. He is the most imaginative, generous and adorable man I know, which makes Jill lucky indeed.

My first experience came when we had invited Kurt to London on a promotion tour. By this time we had published his brilliant book *Slaughterhouse 5* and he was a big celebrity, much in demand by the media. In addition to being an excellent television performer he is a superb lecturer; very funny and serious as well. We had put Kurt and Jill up at the Connaught. Jill grabbed the phone whenever anyone rang their suite and blocked anything she didn't like the sound of. Meanwhile she pursued her own interests. While Kurt was visiting the Cape offices, she came to see me and asked for John Fowles's telephone number. She was filled with admiration for his work, she claimed, and desperately wanted to photograph him. It so happens that John hates to be photographed, which is probably why he had not responded to her approaches. I told her that John had particularly asked us not to give out his number to anyone at all. She argued with me but I did not budge. Immediately she left my office, I rang John warning him that I was sure she would somehow get hold of his number and that he should be prepared. Jill, for her part, walked down the stairs from my office and straight into the Publicity Department where she announced that I had mislaid John's number and had suggested she ask them for it. I am afraid they gave it to her. In spite of the fact that she offered to hire a helicopter and fly down to Lyme Regis to fit in with whatever John's schedule might be, I am happy to say that no photographic session took place.

In New York Kurt would invariably invite me out to dinner and it was almost without exception to Elaine's that we went. It is a tacky but chic Upper East Side restaurant which serves rather indifferent food but is strong on atmosphere. Elaine's has been a success for decades. Kurt is one of the celebrities who frequents the place, though I doubt whether he sees himself as such. The most dependable sighting is Woody Allen who can be found there almost every day. I cannot resist telling another of my favourite Jill Kremetz stories. Bob Gottlieb had an extremely pretty young daughter called Lizzie. Jill rang Bob to say that she would very much like to photograph the child. Bob said he really didn't want her to be photographed, but Jill wore him down, as she tends to, and finally he agreed but on one condition. This was that Jill should promise that the photograph would not be reproduced in any newspaper. Jill agreed. Come the day, she turned up bringing with her a brand-new, ravishing teddy bear. Lizzie played with the bear blissfully and Jill duly took her photographs. When she left, she carried the teddy bear away with her and Lizzie was of course distraught. Two weeks later a large photograph of Lizzie appeared in the *New York Times*. Then, shortly before Christmas, Jill rang Bob's wife, the actress Maria Tucci, and suggested that she might like to give Bob a print of one of her photographs of Lizzie as a Christmas present, adding that she was prepared to let her have it at cost – for a mere $200! The final, happier, chapter was when Joe Heller heard this story. He managed to find the self-same teddy bear and presented it to Lizzie as a Christmas gift. Bob Gottlieb said to Jill the next time he ran into her, 'So you see, it all ended happily.' I doubt whether Jill would have known what he was talking about.

When Kurt left Cape Cod, he bought a house in East Hampton where he feels very much at home, spending a lot of time there while Jill is pursuing her career in New York. Kurt is happy for me to come and stay almost any weekend. He is not attracted to the beach and much prefers to work at home all day. I go off for the day with a picnic and we meet up in the evenings. Kurt is invariably great fun to be with, full of zest, and he appears to see the funny side of life at all times. Yet underneath I know he is a depressive. Most nights there is a party or a dinner to which one or other of us has been invited: we may go to Ed Doctorow's, author of the celebrated *Ragtime*, or Gloria Steinem's.

An especially celebrated party-giver, both in Long Island and in New York, was George Plimton. He was a very tall, good-looking man-about-town, escort of Jackie Kennedy and many other beautiful ladies. He was also a writer and the founder of the literary magazine the *Paris Review*. The magazine is especially famous for its interviews. George commissioned various writers and critics – not necessarily particularly famous ones – to conduct in-depth interviews with leading authors. Many of the interviews turned out to be of the highest quality, so much so that they have even been collected and published in hardback. When I met George in New York he was most flattering about the authors we published at Cape and invited me to become London editor of the *Paris Review*. I cannot say that I have contributed a great deal over the years but I am proud of the title.

I should mention a notorious party given by George in New York some thirty years ago (I must add that I was not present). On this occasion Norman Mailer got extremely drunk and savagely stabbed his wife, who had to be taken to hospital. Meanwhile, the party continued. At a *Paris Review* party I had the pleasure of meeting Norman Mailer and we saw each other on a good number of occasions thereafter.

There is something about his personality that leads me to say that I cannot help feeling flattered that he recognizes me. Whilst Mailer has a belligerent reputation I have always found him to be courteous, even gentle, although he has the physique and the stance of a boxer. I find him attractive and he's certainly one of the most vital of writers. Perhaps I am prejudiced through having been in awe of his work ever since I was a teenager when I read the war novel that made him famous, *The Naked and the Dead*.

One of the East Hampton dinner parties we enjoyed most was a very small one at John Irving's house. He cooked dinner personally and made a memorable figure in his kitchen, standing behind the kitchen counter and swigging back bottle after bottle of beer. John is garrulous and good-looking and has an exceptionally athletic body. That night he produced numerous dishes including delectable scallops and, to finish, a blueberry pie. I had come to the party with Kurt, and I recalled that it was he who had introduced me to John Irving's work some years previously (John's books outsell those of most of his peers). The book in question on this occasion was *The World According to Garp*. Kurt had been sent a proof copy and was so taken with the book that he wanted me to read it right away. At the time I was staying with Bob Gottlieb, who happens to live opposite Kurt on East 48th Street, and so Kurt slipped the proof through the letterbox. I could not stop reading and rang the agent the following day. I was tremendously excited. Alas, I learned that the British rights had already been sold to Liz Calder at Gollancz. When Liz subsequently joined us, I'm delighted to say that John Irving came with her.

To return to John's party: Kurt was freewheeling in conversation with Joe Heller. Kurt was in great form and started talking about a lavish wedding he had been to that afternoon. He was in awe of the extravagance of the event and said,

'Imagine, the tent alone cost twenty thousand dollars for just one evening.'

'How do you know that?' someone asked.

'I'm married to a lady called Jill Kremetz,' came the reply.

JOHN FOWLES

THE LETTER CAME FROM James Kinross, a small London literary agency. The message was brief: 'I am sending you herewith a book called *The Collector* by John Fowles. I hope you like it. I look forward to hearing.' It was left to me to inform Mr Kinross, whom I had never met, that I not only liked the book but the author was outstandingly talented and likely to have a glorious future, which would go far beyond *The Collector*.

I was impatient to meet John Fowles. This was not difficult to arrange since it transpired he lived in Hampstead, where he taught at St Godrick's School, close to his home. Two days later he came to see me at Bedford Square. It was a grey, rainy day and he was wearing a dingy, damp mackintosh. The coat was unbuttoned and he appeared disinclined to take it off. I told John how very much I had admired *The Collector* and then, without further ado, I asked the question which most preoccupied me: 'Is this your first book?'

The answer came back immediately: 'Good God, no.'

'You have written others?'

'Yes.'

'How many?'

'Nine.'

'You mean you have written nine other novels from cover to cover?'

'Oh yes.'

'And what happened to these books?'

'I sent one of them to two publishers.' John's manner was a mixture of diffidence and conceit. Being a schoolmaster could make him appear pedantic at times.

Years later I discovered that of the nine manuscripts two were totally rewritten and published as *The Magus* and *The French Lieutenant's Woman*. As for the rest, we shall never know. John's wife Elizabeth told me that shortly before they moved out of Underhill Farm in Dorset to take up residence in Belmont House at the top of Lyme Regis, she watched smoke rise for several days from the chimney in the hut at the bottom of the garden where John used to work. Certainly Elizabeth had never read any of these manuscripts. Nor, as far as I know, had anyone else. John made a practice of not showing work in progress to anyone. Not even to his wife.

The Collector made an exceptional mark for a first novel, especially in America. Throughout his career John Fowles has been more successful, both critically and commercially, in the States than in England. Given the fact that hundreds of thousands of serious English readers greatly admire his work, it has always puzzled me that he should not be more highly rated by British critics. When the leading English novelists are discussed, the name of John Fowles is, strangely, not included.

The Collector was followed by *The Magus*, a magical mystery set in John's beloved Greece, on the island of Spetsos. There he was employed as a teacher at an English boarding school and there he fell in love with the wife of a fellow teacher, a man, furthermore, who was his best friend and, to make matters worse, an aspiring and unpublished novelist. John has always been prone to feelings of guilt; the act of falling in love with a best friend's wife would be enough to make anyone suffer these.

In the sixties we used to have infinitely closer relations with our reps than publishers do today. So when Andrew Jaffrey Smith, our Scottish rep, asked me whether there was any chance of John Fowles giving a talk at Smith's (no relation) Bookshop in Glasgow, I put the idea to John. I was acquainted with Willie Andersen, the manager of Smith's, and knew him to be a serious fiction reader as well as a particular Fowles fan. John said he didn't mind going to Scotland but was not willing to give a prepared talk. He suggested instead that he and I might do an 'in conversation with' as we had done elsewhere. I was happy to accompany John, so we fixed a date and booked our flight tickets and hotel. Needless to say, Cape paid for all of this. When I learned that Smith's were selling tickets for the event, I couldn't help thinking they might have offered to pay our expenses. They sold 200-odd tickets and, even after clearing half the shop, they were unable to accommodate more than that number. They must have turned away at least a further 100 customers on the night.

Our evening was a triumph. John was in great form and the questions were unusually intelligent. A total of 300 books were sold, mainly copies of *The Magus* and almost all in hardcover. Our audience departed well satisfied and eight people remained – John, Andrew Jaffrey Smith and me, plus Willie and four members of his staff. By now it was 8.30 p.m. and there followed some shuffling with regard to dinner. I found it hard to believe, but Willie asked me if I had made a reservation. Perhaps this could be seen as no more than astute business practice. I said a firm no, whereupon he suggested two or three rather fancy restaurants. I felt that Cape had already made an extremely worthy contribution and was not prepared to throw in an expensive dinner for eight. So I said I had passed a couple of places while walking from our hotel to the bookshop and suggested we stroll along and check them out. We spent an enjoyable and drunken evening in one of them. At just before midnight, when the restaurant was about to close, we were presented with a bill. I let it sit on the table for a few minutes until it became fully apparent that Willie was not going to pick it up, at which point I did so. This was in the late sixties. Since then Willie has become one of our most eminent booksellers.

By the time of the publication of *The Magus* my first wife, Fay, and I had become close friends of John and Elizabeth Fowles and we spent many weekends together at Lyme. Sometimes it is difficult not to be critical of one's friends, especially when they seem to be mean. That is how it was between us and the Fowleses. Each time we stayed in their beautiful home, Belmont House, we would be irritated anew by the fact that baths were to be taken between 5 and 7 p.m., the period during which the hot water was switched on (and I believe still is). Equally strange was the fact that whilst John loved good wine he only very rarely served a bottle that came from anywhere other than a local store or even a supermarket. Most bizarrely of all, though, he once sent my daughter (and his god-daughter) Hannah a half-used box of crayons for her birthday. This was *so* bizarre that we imagined it must have been some kind of error.

John's preoccupation with money applied not only to others but equally to himself. He had a dilapidated old greenhouse, and given his passion for plants and the very considerable monies he had made from the film rights in *The French Lieutenant's Woman* (of which more later), I suggested that he treat himself to a new one. He said in that pained way he had, 'Oh, Tom, if you knew what a greenhouse costs!' In my ignorance I shrugged and he went on, 'It would cost between one thousand five hundred and two thousand pounds.' He clearly considered this a prohibitive expense.

One day John asked if Fay and I might like to join him and Elizabeth on a trip to the Scilly Isles. And so we booked

ourselves into the Island Hotel on Tresco. John had long loved
the place. It was a birdwatcher's paradise and he shared his
knowledge freely. To watch John's excitement at recognizing
birds and their sounds was a daily joy. We arrived in Tresco
via St Mary's, the capital island of the Scillies. There John
announced that he wanted to 'pop into Gibson's'. He said
it in a manner that implied that the whole world must surely
know what he was talking about. I fell straight into the trap
and asked, 'What is Gibson's?' It turned out to be an ancient
stationery store. For four generations the shop had belonged
to a family of photographers and throughout the years they
had photographed shipwrecks off the Scilly Isles. Even today
they continue to make photographic prints from the original
glass plates. John was keen to add to his collection and I could
not resist buying a few prints as well. The pictures were
beautiful and John began to tell us the enthralling stories
behind each wreck. It was as if we were listening to a series of
plots by John Fowles and I was so fascinated by the material
that I hit on the idea of publishing a book of photographs to
be captioned by John. This was the birth of the book we called
Shipwreck.

Two years later John had finished his third novel, *The
French Lieutenant's Woman*. There was always a mystery as to

when he would complete a book. He seemed to make a point of keeping even his beloved publisher in the dark. On this occasion, when the book was ready, he rang to ask whether he could come to see me. This meant a journey up from Lyme Regis, which was a rare event since John disliked London intensely. He brought the manuscript with him, placed it on the corner of my enormous desk and said, 'This is a book you won't like.' How wrong he was. *The French Lieutenant's Woman* was simply the most magnificent piece of storytelling I had read for many years. I say this in spite of the fact that it has a double layer, as it were, for part of the book is set in the Victorian era and part in modern times. It also has a double ending, literally two completely different endings, and amazingly, none of this appears the least bit contrived.

I telephoned John immediately to express my admiration, and even in this first call I could not resist saying that the book would make a superb film. Nor could I help putting down the film of *The Magus*. True, *The Magus* is a particularly complex book, but that does not excuse an unintelligible film with banal performances from Michael Caine, Candice Bergen and Anthony Quinn. I am confident it was one of the worst films I have ever seen. I insisted that in the case of *The French Lieutenant's Woman*, it was John's first duty to 'protect' the novel. This means, quite simply, not selling out, and by not selling out, I meant that John should sell no more than an option, no matter how much money he was offered for the rights.

'But what', John asked, 'if my agent comes up with an offer of, say, a million dollars?'

'You decline,' I said cheerfully.

John was unsure. It wasn't that he wanted the money, more that he found the prospect of refusing an embarrassment.

'The only important issue is the ultimate quality of the film. Retaining control means having a say in the choice of director, choice of writer and possibly even the choice of actors,' I went on.

John was obviously worried. And then he had an idea. 'Would you be willing to help?' he asked. This to someone who had at the beginning of his career attempted to work in the cinema was a dream come true. I did not want a penny from John. My involvement would be entirely on behalf of his book and I was tremendously excited.

Rather than simply waiting for unsolicited interest, I put my mind to thinking of directors with the intelligence and the talent to do the book justice. The first person I decided to approach was Karel Reisz, who happened to live three houses down the road from me in Chalcot Gardens. I dropped off the book, which was still in manuscript. Alas, the timing was bad. Karel had just made a costume drama, namely *Isadora* with Vanessa Redgrave, and he was disinclined to go straight on to another.

My next choice I considered a long shot. It was Lindsay Anderson, who had directed *This Sporting Life* with Richard Harris. Again I drew a blank. Lindsay didn't really respond to the book and so that was that.

I must have approached half a dozen others, including Dick Lester who seemed to have the right sense of style and invention. Among them I found one director ready to get seriously engaged and that was Fred Zinneman, famous especially for *High Noon*. He was crazy about *The French Lieutenant's Woman* and talked of it as his next film. He raised the money to commission a screenplay without difficulty; his standing was such that there was no shortage of studios prepared to back him. Fred's choice of writer was Dennis Potter but the screenplay Potter wrote disappointed him and he became discouraged, reluctantly deciding not to proceed.

By now John was also in danger of becoming despondent. We had been at it for more than two years, and although I was as determined as ever, I thought perhaps we should change tack. Given the fact that the screenplay appeared to be the main problem, I suggested to John we approach a screenwriter, and someone capable of solving our problem. My first choice was Harold Pinter. I was not at all convinced that the book would appeal to him but it was worth a try. Within a week Harold rang me, filled with enthusiasm. But there was a new snag. He had recently been commissioned to write a screenplay of Proust for Joseph Losey, obviously no overnight task. As it turned out, the film was never made but it prevented Harold from seriously considering *The French Lieutenant's Woman*.

We flash forward a further four years. I was coming out of my house in Chalcot Gardens when Karel Reisz strolled by. I had not seen him for a while and asked what he was working on. He said there were several possible projects but he particularly hoped to work on something with Harold. There was no need to ask 'Harold who?' I took the opportunity of mentioning that the book I had shown Karel six years previously had been admired by Pinter. 'Perhaps it might be a possibility for the two of you.' Karel was sceptical but I was insistent: 'Why don't you call Harold right now and see how he feels?' Somewhat reluctantly Karel went into his study and made the call while I waited in the kitchen with his wife Betsy. When Karel came out it was to say that he and Harold had arranged to meet the following Monday.

Their Monday meeting went well and Karel and Harold agreed to start work. It was my task to negotiate a fee with Harold's agent, Jimmy Wax. My next call was to John Calley at Warner Brothers. Calley had always believed in the book and indicated to me that, with the right ingredients, Warner would want to go ahead. The prospect of Reisz and Pinter delighted him and he approved Harold's fee. He came up with the following, classically Hollywood, statement: 'Bob Shapiro [Head of Production] and I can't come over tomorrow but we'll come the day after.' They were in Los Angeles and yet it sounded like catching a local bus. At this point there was really nothing further to discuss and their journey seemed unnecessary, but they were determined to come.

For the first time in nine years the film appeared to be a probability. Calley's visit gave me a good opportunity to discuss my own position. I asked him what title he thought appropriate. In his typically laidback manner, he asked me what title *I* would like. I asked for the most impressive title he felt justified. His answer was: 'Executive Producer.' That sounded good to me. When, I told Karel he said that he found it ridiculously elevated to the point of being unacceptable. 'Associate Producer' was the highest title which made sense to him and so I settled for that.

Karel and Harold met regularly and the writing went well. Meanwhile, Karel made a momentous contribution. He offered the part of Sarah to Meryl Streep. It wasn't just that Meryl accepted, she fell in love with the project. The script was close to being finished and Karel sent a copy to Calley. Back came a telegram stating that it was one of the greatest scripts Calley had ever read.

Karel now began to prepare a preliminary budget. This went off to Los Angeles three weeks after the script. The budget was for $8 million. Calley's response was that unless Karel could bring the film in for $6 million it was 'off'. This task was impossible. I could not restrain myself from phoning Calley for some explanation. He said to me: 'You must take into consideration the fact that this is an art movie.' I pointed out that Warner had commissioned a film of *The French Lieutenant's Woman* scripted by Harold Pinter (and, furthermore, brilliantly scripted according to Calley) and directed by Karel Reisz – in other words, if it was an art film now it must surely have been so all along. He was intransigent and we were obliged to put the film into what is known in Hollywood as 'turnaround', and so it became our task to find another distributor willing to finance the film and, incidentally, to repay Warner their outlay.

To make matters worse we had lost invaluable time. By now it was March, and we had one month to start shooting in order to complete the film before the summer madness of Lyme Regis. It was a tough assignment. I recall thinking that if the film fell through at this late stage, even I might not have the energy to begin afresh.

It did not come to this. We found an unexpected ally in Sam Shaw, Meryl's agent. So keen was Meryl to play in the film that she had not only granted us extra time but also asked Sam to help. An agent as well connected as Sam Shaw wields a lot of power and within a short period he'd managed to arrange a transfer to United Artists.

Shooting the film was almost an anticlimax compared to bringing it about. Inexperienced as I was, I derived considerable satisfaction from playing the producer. Karel was exceedingly generous in welcoming my presence both for the filming and when it came to watching the rushes at the end of each day.

The one function I felt qualified to perform was that of publicist. My first task in that department was to take care of Lord Snowdon when he came down to shoot Meryl. He wanted to photograph her on the undercliff and she wanted to be shot on the Cobb in order not to waste time travelling. I was determined to hold out on her behalf but Meryl gave in and Snowdon got his way. I was present during the photo session and found him surprisingly nervous. Later we had a row. He told me it was my job to make Meryl available for whatever he required. I told him that as far as I was concerned, my job was to take care of Meryl. He was not a happy man.

The Snowdon episode was followed by another embarrassment. This was a story in the *Daily Mail*, according to which

I was busy looking for a studio for Meryl's husband, who is a sculptor. The paper claimed I wanted to make sure that he was as far away as possible so that I could the more readily pursue my affair with Meryl. I telephoned our lawyer, Michael Rubinstein, and asked whether I had a case. 'Absolutely not,' he said. 'The suggestion that you are having an affair with Meryl Streep is nothing but a compliment.'

As we approached the end of shooting I began the serious part of my job – the task of promotion. I asked United Artists whether they wished me to be selective or whether they wanted as much publicity as possible. They looked blank. I explained: 'We have five colour supplements in England. Is the goal to have stories in all five? Or just to choose the most desirable?' The answer was to go for all five, although United Artists considered this an inconceivable achievement. By thinking in editorial terms, as opposed to simply handing out the usual film promotional material, I came up with five totally different stories; furthermore, in the case of two of the newspapers I negotiated a fee. I asked for the cheques to be made out to United Artists. But when I forwarded the money they were totally bemused. They had never before been paid for a story and had nowhere to place such monies. Of course, I didn't care about the money one way or the other. My rationale was simply that if you sell something you will be taken more seriously than if you give it away.

The big 'opening day' approached. Karel dislikes any form of razzmatazz and so the Cannes Film Festival, for example, would have been out of the question. He also dislikes British premières, royal or otherwise. He chose to see the film at the Odeon Haymarket, where he bought seven tickets at the box office. It was the reaction of the public that interested him. And so Karel, his wife Betsy, Meryl Streep, Jeremy Irons, Harold Pinter, Antonia Fraser and I went to the cinema together. It seemed a strange way to celebrate. At the end, the titles came on the screen. There was my name alongside 'Associate Producer'. In a sense I felt completely irrelevant to the film we had just seen, and yet in another sense I had played an absolutely essential role, since but for me the film we had just seen would never have been made.

CRITICS

STYLE IN NON-FICTION has always been as important to me as it is in fiction, and that is how I came to approach three outstanding critics: Clive James, Bernard Levin and Kenneth Tynan.

CLIVE JAMES

Clive was an Australian who at the age of thirty-three became the television critic of the *Observer*, which was where I read him. It was where everyone read him. His prose was dazzling and each Sunday he would come up with a number of gems making his review a joy. Obviously one does not read TV criticism in order to decide whether to view a programme but purely for the pleasure of it. To publish a book of television reviews entails the inclusion of some pieces which are several years old. And yet, to the bemusement of my colleagues, I felt they were so good that this is what I thought we should do. The first collection was called *Visions Before Midnight* and it sold 700 copies. (The break-even figure for an average book is 3,000 copies.) We followed Clive's first book of criticism with a second. And then we were richly rewarded, beyond our wildest dreams, because Clive wrote an autobiographical book, taking the reader up to the age of seventeen. It was called

Unreliable Memoirs and it sold 80,000 copies in hardback alone. Of course I had not had the remotest idea that Clive would ever write such a book. Nor had he.

We went on to publish other volumes of TV criticism, books of essays, novels, books of verse and also further auto-biographical books. One book of verse sold exceptionally well. It was called *Charles Charming's Challenges on the Pathway to the Throne.* I commissioned Marc Boxer, the cartoonist, to illustrate the book and he did so to superb effect. One of Marc's drawings, the one of Prince Charles, gave me an idea. This was to manufacture a mug with Charles's exceptionally large ear forming the handle. On one side of the mug we used Marc's drawing and on the other a verse from Clive's text. I had devised the mug as a purely promotional piece but the demand was so great that we produced several thousand for sale. The final accolade came when Lord Snowdon chose our little mug as one of the prize souvenirs of Charles and Diana's wedding.

Clive and I were close in a way, but our closeness tended to manifest itself on the telephone. It was there that we discussed details of his publishing career, including editorial matters. Within a few years of our first book of his TV criticism, Clive had become a celebrated television personality. Whenever I spoke to him he seemed somewhat frantic and breathless. I did manage to lure him out for lunch a few times, but no more than that. He found it more tempting to take Princess Diana to Le Caprice. One can hardly blame him. Nor do I blame him for leaving Cape once I decided to spend half the year in France. The letter he wrote me was a most elegant piece of work. Elegant and sincere as well.

BERNARD LEVIN

When I wrote to Bernard Levin proposing we publish a collection of his celebrated pieces from *The Times* he came up with a response that impressed me. He said he would love to be published by me, and the idea of a collection certainly appealed to him. But first, he insisted, 'I must write a real book.' This process took him several years, during which I repeatedly offered the collection, but the other book was an absolute point of principle for Bernard. Then, finally, he came up with *The Pendulum Years*.

Prior to publishing Bernard, I had always thought of him as somewhat forbidding. Once I got to know him I found a model author. He was always punctual and always reliable. And the aloof figure of old turned into a warm and considerate friend. Unlike many other authors, who can be an egocentric lot, Bernard was interested in me personally as well as professionally. On the other hand he disliked talking about himself and he most certainly declined to talk about his private life, meaning the ladies in his life. Such things were totally private. He remained a bachelor.

We rarely saw Bernard socially but I recall a dinner party he especially relished. The other guests were Uri Geller and his wife. Uri was telling a story about a beautiful American lady with whom he had had lunch. She wore some particularly expensive antique gold drop earrings. Uri looked at her across the table and then at the earrings. They melted and clattered on to her plate. Shortly after he told this story I observed that the gold bridge in my mouth had come loose. It had been put in place some ten years previously.

In Fleet Street Bernard was a highly regarded figure, always expressing his opinions forcefully and effectively in his column. Whether in agreement or not, one had to admire the manner in which he presented a case. Bernard had Alzheimer's. This would be a terrible affliction for anyone but for someone with as active a mind as Bernard it must have been horrendous.

KENNETH TYNAN

Kenneth Tynan began to write for the *Observer* at the age of twenty-seven. By the time I met him (in 1956) he was already the greatest drama critic of our time, acclaimed as much for his style as for his judgements. Our meeting came about because I telephoned saying I had a project I very much wanted to discuss with him. This resulted in my going to his Mount Street flat. I hoped he might contribute an essay to the book I was editing at the time, *Declaration*. I must say that I was immensely surprised when he agreed and even more so when he told me he thought the venture most worthwhile. I had feared that he might be put off by some of the other contributors, especially Colin Wilson (author of *The Outsider*), whom he regarded as an absurd figure.

We met frequently at the Royal Court, where for several years I attended almost every play. And we also met on the Aldermaston March. This was a march of protest from London to the nuclear reactor at Aldermaston. It was attended by several thousand socialist intellectuals, especially those working in the arts. They included Doris Lessing, Robert Bolt, Christopher Logue, Arnold Wesker and Michael Foot. When Ken recognized me – he did not always do so – he appeared pleased to see me. Subsequently I found myself on his party list. Ken was first married to Elaine Dundy, a zany American lady who wrote a spirited novel, *The Dud Avocado*, and then a marvellously funny autobiography. Elaine drank far too much. When their marriage broke up and she returned to the States, Ken married Kathleen. She was cool and many thought beautiful.

Kathleen would ring me: 'Tom, we're having a party on Friday and very much hope you can come.' Me: 'Oh, thank you, I would love to' (or something to that effect). And then Kathleen: 'By the way, if Kurt Vonnegut is in town, please do feel free to bring him.' She knew perfectly well that Kurt Vonnegut *was* in town. This kind of thing was a frequent occurrence, but there were also occasions when I was invited in my own right. Either way their parties were glamorous and not to be missed. At one of them I found myself talking, together with my wife Fay, who was heavily pregnant, to Ava Gardner. Suddenly she pointed to Fay's stomach: 'The first was a girl, so was the second, and this one is a boy.' She got it absolutely right. She was not called 'the witch' for nothing.

Ken was a tremendous enthusiast and a natural campaigner. We were living in the days of the Lord Chamberlain. Plays had to be submitted to him and he was for ever insisting upon deletions of seemingly harmless bits which he considered obscene. So, Ken had an idea. It was to put on a show with acts by various anonymous hands. He called the show *Oh, Calcutta!*. The authors were the best writers Ken knew, that is, the best in the land. Even Samuel Beckett contributed. The plan was that the pieces should be of an overtly sexual nature and so provoke the Lord Chamberlain into closing the show, at which point Ken would do battle. Obviously, under these circumstances, it was not easy to raise money, and so Ken called upon his friends to invest. For this purpose I most certainly counted as one of them. I invested £500. The show opened at the Round House and, to everybody's amazement, the Lord Chamberlain did not close it. Then, to our even greater amazement, *Oh, Calcutta!* transferred to the West End where it ran for many years. It was an extremely low-cost production and therefore inordinately profitable. My modest investment earned a great deal of money – £20,000.

Given my admiration for Ken's writing, I wish I had been

able to publish more of his work. His essays were as special in their way as his theatre criticism. I remember one on Valencia which he wrote for the *New Yorker*. Before reading it you might not have had any desire to visit Valencia, but Ken brought the city alive in an amazing way. He made it irresistible. We published a book of his essays and I also commissioned his autobiography, which would have enthralled a large number of readers. He signed the contract and took the advance, but he never delivered.

LATIN AMERICA

MY VERY FIRST VENTURE into the Latin American field falls firmly into the category of luck, which in this case could be called prodigious luck. Shortly after the Cuban revolution I was invited by the Casa de Las Americas (the cultural body of Cuba) to pay a visit to the country, all expenses paid. On arriving in Havana I discovered that I was one of a panel of judges chosen to select the best Spanish-language novel of the year. To my embarrassment I could not read Spanish (although I speak a little), but no one had bothered to check with me, nor even to tell me the purpose of the invitation. I asked whether I might none the less attend the judging sessions. This presented no problem at all. There was a particular title that came up frequently in discussion, *No One Writes to the Colonel*. It was not a novel but a collection of stories, a first book by an unknown Colombian writer. The name of the author was Gabriel García Márquez.

When, three weeks later, I returned to London I immediately made some enquiries. It turned out that the agent for García Márquez was Carmen Barcells, who then represented most Latin American writers. After much haggling we came to an unprecedented agreement. We signed a contract for the stories as part of a five-book agreement. Publishing novels in translation is so speculative, and usually so unprofitable, that I have never before, nor since, contracted for more than one book at a time. *No One Writes to the Colonel* was, according to my reports, a fine book, but it was not an amazing one. So one might well ask, why this unprecedented deal? It will become apparent in due course.

The first time I met García Márquez was in London. I knew he had been there for some time and had expected him to ring me. Finally he did. I asked him how long he had been in London and he said three months. Then I asked how much longer he was staying and he said two days. I asked why he had not called earlier and he replied that it was because he wanted to speak to me in English. But his English remained exceedingly broken and we quickly switched to French, whereupon I succeeded in persuading him to come to lunch the following day.

Although he appeared to be vague, it turned out that he had a precise knowledge of our publishing history. He was well aware of the five-book contract and the fact that his books had not done well in England. He came up with a memorable statement: 'Do not worry about money,' he said. 'My next book will make history. It will sell and sell and sell.' He did not sound the least bit arrogant; he was merely sharing a conviction. The book, the fifth in our contract, was *One Hundred Years of Solitude*. And now, of course, the contract made excellent sense.

When I next saw Gabo, as he is known to his friends, *One Hundred Years of Solitude* had been published and he had the status of a god in Latin America. His books were on sale not only in bookshops but also at news-stands. They were read by everyone in South America. I mean from university professors to road sweepers. I have never known such a phenomenon in relation to a work of literature.

On Gabo's subsequent visit to England I am happy to say he gave us some days' notice and we were able to arrange a small dinner in his honour. We invited him and Mercedes, his wife, to arrive a little ahead of the others. While we had him to ourselves I took the opportunity of showing Gabo a small trophy of which I was rather proud. It was an extremely rare proof copy of *One Hundred Years of Solitude*. I asked him to sign it and he did so reluctantly, but adding in that mock-serious way of his that he had asked his publisher to print a facsimile edition of 10,000 copies in order to 'put an end to all this nonsense'. 'That', he said, pointing to my copy, 'is worth five thousand dollars.'

I seem to be moving from meal to meal but that is how it was on the occasions we met. The next meal I shared with Gabo was hosted by the King of Sweden in his banqueting hall in Stockholm, to celebrate García Márquez having won the Nobel Prize for Literature. Unfortunately I was placed far away from my author but that did not diminish the pleasure and the pride I felt. To make up for our separation at the dinner, I spent most of the following day in and out of Gabo's hotel suite. There I participated in a constant festivity, with Gabo holding court. The majority of those in his suite were Cubans and they had arranged for various tapas to be imported. Later I heard that Gabo had not so much as greeted any of his other publishers, not even the Swedish one. Although I felt honoured to have been given special treatment I felt embarrassed for the others. At the same time I must admit that I was flattered when Gabo introduced me as the only publisher (apart from his Spanish language house) who had published all his books.

A couple of years after the Nobel celebrations Regina and I were planning a visit to Mexico and so I rang Gabo. Over the years I had rung him many times but had never, not on a single occasion, been successful in reaching him. This time the gods were with me and he answered the telephone himself. He asked which days we would be in Mexico City. There was a choice of two and he invited us to lunch on one of them, suggesting we arrive at twelve noon. Lunch began at about one. It ended at 8 p.m. It was the most memorable lunch I have ever experienced. And not, of course, simply for the food, which was the most delicious kind of home cooking including every variety of *molé*. We were offered course after course after course, and Gabo's children and his grandchildren and his great-grandchildren were woven in and out of the meal. In between courses Regina and I strolled with our host around the garden, which formed an inner courtyard to the house. I recall asking Gabo, who lived in a suburb of the city about an hour by taxi from the centre, whether he ever missed city life. He said, 'No, because if I lived in the city I would miss being outside it.' At eight we left with a big bear hug for Gabo and another for Mercedes. In spite of all the affection, and so much intimacy, I knew that I would be fortunate if I saw him again on more than just one or two occasions.

*

I WAS GABO'S first publisher in England, as I was that of the Peruvian writer Mario Vargas Llosa. I had read American reviews of his first novel, *The Time of the Hero*, and was able to buy the British rights. Mario spent a good deal of time in London each year and we quickly became friends. He was at all times warm and smiling and was also, according to my wife, extremely good-looking. He was always unusually well dressed. He told me that to be published by Cape meant a great deal to him, which of course made me feel good. He wrote a massive study on the work of García Márquez, a book of 1,000 pages. The two were good friends at the time, but when Mario decided to run for President of Peru, he became extremely right-wing. Gabo, who is on the far left, and a close friend of Castro, could not forgive him. We published several further books of Mario's and then he wrote an 800-page novel called *The Cathedral*. Having lost money on most of the other far shorter novels, I am afraid I did not have the courage to take it on.

*

IN THE CASE OF Carlos Fuentes, the Mexican novelist, I didn't publish his very first book although given the opportunity I would happily have done so. A copy was handed to me by his then publisher in America, a strange figure called Ivan Obolensky. Shortly thereafter, and with great enthusiasm, I took Carlos on. Early in our friendship he spoke of his desire to take me to Mexico on one of his many trips, leaving it to me to suggest a date. Finally we made our plans and arranged to meet in Oaxaca, where there is a famous hotel that was previously a convent. It seemed like the place to stay, although I gathered that it was extremely difficult to obtain a reservation. Carlos simply said that accommodation would present no problem. There is something so worldly about Carlos that I cannot imagine a trifle such as a hotel reservation ever presenting a problem. He mentioned that we would be joined by Rose and Bill Styron, which, since they were old friends, made it even more of a family affair.

On our first night Carlos had arranged for us to have dinner with the Governor at his home. We were collected from the hotel by limousine and escorted by a police motorcade. I thought this a bit odd. The limousine journey took half an hour and on foot it would have taken a few minutes. At dinner I was seated next to a very handsome-looking woman, introduced to me as Jean Smith. The name meant nothing to me, and in my ignorance, I asked her what she did. Regina sat opposite and I could see her squirming. Jean Smith turned out to be the sister of John F. Kennedy, and furthermore her son had recently been on trial for rape, a case which was covered nightly on American television over a period of months. I gathered that she had come on the trip to Mexico to recover from the strain. After dinner I asked Carlos if it would be in order for me to walk back to the hotel – I simply couldn't face the motorcade again. Everyone, including Jean Smith, in whose honour the security had clearly been laid on, walked with me.

*

ANOTHER OF THE great Latin American writers whom I published was the Argentinian, Borges. We were not his only publishers and I never got to know him at all well. In the sixties Borges was extremely fashionable and very widely read, especially among younger readers. For many years he wrote only poetry and then in his late fifties he began to write prose. I recall asking him what had brought about this change. I shall never forget his answer. Apparently he had had a serious fall and had hit his head. For several months he suffered from concussion and was unable to write. Then, when he was partially recovered, he was still afraid that he might never be able to write again. So he had an idea. It was to attempt to write prose, his reasoning being that if he were unable to do so, this might simply be an indication that he did not have the gift for prose, but his return to writing poetry would remain a possibility.

*

HAVING BEEN CALLED Mr Latin American Literature by Carlos Fuentes, I should mention some of the other Latin American writers I published. They include the novelist Asturias, who won the Nobel Prize in 1967, the essayist Octavio Paz, who won the prize in 1990, and the poet Pablo Neruda, who won it in 1971. I have written about Neruda at some small length elsewhere. With these mentions of the Nobel Prize and of 'my authors' having won it, I am proud to say that this has occurred eleven times since 1963. It is worth adding that a number of publishers seem to view the prize as some kind of trophy which is awarded to them rather than to their authors. I too naturally find it satisfying when an author of ours wins, but my delight is in direct relation to the role I have played in their lives. In Nobel terms, alas, English writers rarely find favour with the Swedish academy. The last one to do so was William Golding. The writer who has been most frequently mentioned in recent times, and invariably passed over, is Graham Greene. The deliberations of the Nobel Committee are kept admirably secret, but based on what I have been told by several Swedish publishers I would favour the following theory for Greene's exclusion. It appears that he had an affair with Anita Björk, a very beautiful Swedish actress. She was married to a much-loved Swedish poet called Stig Dagerman. He committed suicide by putting his head in a gas oven (presumably in distress at his wife's conduct). Graham Greene chose the very same method of suicide for his play *The Potting Shed*.

One final point I wish to make about the Nobel Prize is that it is tremendously highly rated in most countries and frequently transforms the career of a writer. Sales may double or even increase as much as tenfold. In England, to put it bluntly, the reading public does not give a damn.

JOHN LENNON

PUBLISHING IS SO OFTEN a matter of luck. It would be difficult to cite a better example than the following. I had commissioned a book on pop music – a subject of which I am singularly ignorant. The author, a young man called Michael Braun, came every now and then to my office to discuss progress. One day he brought with him a few scraps of letter paper from various hotels in Brighton, Manchester and Glasgow. They were covered with handwritten verses and line drawings. As I looked at them I was instantly amused by their humour and their originality. The best of them made me laugh aloud. 'Who on earth did these?' I asked. The answer was: 'John Lennon.' Apparently, during an interview, John had mentioned his hobby of writing and drawing what he called 'doodles'. He showed a few to Braun and here they were. Of course this excited me and I knew immediately that I would want to publish them if only Lennon would produce enough for a book.

My first priority was to meet the man himself. An arrangement was made for me to attend a concert at the Wimbledon Southern Area Fan Club. After the concert I was taken backstage where the four Beatles stood next to one another behind an iron grille. At the bottom of the grille there was a narrow space and it was through this that the fans pushed their programmes and scraps of paper which they hoped their idols might sign. I was shown through a back door into the area where the boys were standing. From there I watched the frenzy. John was hastily introduced to me but at this point he had no time to talk, and so I sat and waited. The signing ritual continued for well over an hour during which the fans filed by, one by one, with their offerings. As they passed, many of them keeled over and were piled into one of the waiting ambulances to be revived.

Finally the moment arrived when I could speak to John calmly. He was clearly flattered by the fact that I liked what he had written. But he was bemused by my professional interest, since he considered his writing to be nothing but light-hearted scribbles. In his sardonic way John managed to make me feel slightly foolish for being impressed by his frivolity. This attitude notwithstanding, there began that evening as pleasurable a publisher–author relationship as I have experienced. The pieces I first saw represented a small proportion of *John Lennon in His Own Write*, as the book came to be called. In the months that followed I coaxed John into producing the balance of his slim volume. On occasion I felt the need to persuade him to drop a particular piece that did not seem good enough, but I was always conscious of the fact that if I were too harsh John might well abandon the project altogether.

Normally authors visited me in Bedford Square and we worked in the peace of my office. John, however, avoided going out whenever possible and so I went to the flat just off the Cromwell Road that he shared with Paul, Ringo and George. To get there I would have to fight my way through several hundred fans waiting at the front door of the building. Inside, John's place was like a playground filled with unruly children, but in spite of the pandemonium we always managed to find a relatively quiet corner. It wasn't easy to work under those conditions.

I remember one occasion when I went to see John, taking

with me a copy of a cartoon book that we were publishing. The drawings were by Mel Calman and they seemed to me to bear a remote relationship to John's own work. I thought he might like them enough to allow me to quote him. It was the only time I asked anything of John. He leafed through the drawings at great speed, looked me in the face through those famous glasses, and said: 'Why don't you suggest he take up the guitar?'

The time had come to negotiate a contract and John suggested I talk to Brian Epstein. Epstein not only discovered the Beatles but managed their lives in every detail. I was expecting him to be tough and to demand a large advance. In the taxi on my way to his office I speculated that perhaps he would want a £100,000. In fact the tycoon I had prepared myself for was concerned only about the manner in which the book would be published. Brian was most charming. It was incidentally rumoured that he had a crush on John and this may well be so. Whilst not conventionally handsome there was certainly something very sexy about his young protégée.

The advance we agreed on was £10,000. It turned out to be irrelevant in that we sold 400,000 copies in the UK and about the same in America plus several translated editions. This, despite the number of puns which one might have thought would make the book untranslatable. Strangely enough, John's fame notwithstanding, booksellers were suspicious of the sales potential. I persuaded our Sales Manager to make a lightning journey around the country in order to up the advance sales, but even so we subscribed a mere 20,000 copies. However, from the moment of publication, which was in 1964, the book became a colossal success both in the literary and in the commercial sense. The demand for the book was such that on the Monday after publication I arrived at my office at 9 a.m. to find a dozen booksellers queuing at our warehouse which at the time, was located in a mews behind Bedford Square.

These men were so desperate for re-orders that they came personally. It is something that has never happened to me before or since.

In the *Sunday Times* John was compared at considerable length to Edward Lear, and in the *Observer* to no less illustrious a figure than Lewis Carroll. I am convinced that if his book had been published in a more predictable manner, with, for example, a picture of him playing his guitar on the cover in place of the portrait we used, these extraordinary reviews might not have materialized. As things turned out we achieved the best of all possible worlds. Not only did the book sell in phenomenal numbers, it put John on the literary map.

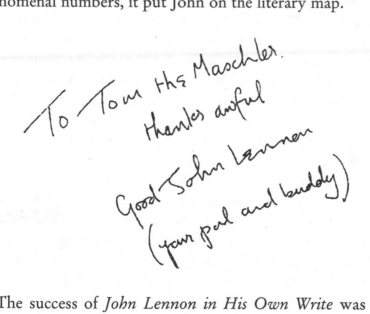

The success of *John Lennon in His Own Write* was such that I inevitably proposed a second volume. It was to be a similar mix of verse and drawings. This time John did not have a title to hand and so I asked him to make some suggestions. Authors frequently have a hard time choosing an original title. In John's case he delighted in the experience and within twenty-four hours he had come up with a number of superb suggestions. For example: *Stop One and Buy Me*, *The Transistor Negro*, and, of course, the one we chose, *A Spaniard in the Works*. The book sold as well as *In His Own Write*, which is most unusual for a second book.

Not long after publication John rang to ask if he could come to my office in order to introduce me to a friend who had written a book. The book was called *Grapefruit* and I did not take to it. I did not take to the author either. Her name was Yoko Ono. It saddened me to see John so clearly infatuated with someone as cool and apparently humourless as Ono. Shortly afterwards, he left his adorable wife Cyn and began 'one of the great love affairs of our time'. Even many of those closest to John were bemused. For my part, I only met Yoko on one other occasion and that was in the Dakota, not long after John's death. Visiting her was rather like entering the inner sanctum of a Mafia chief. The walls seemed dark, the lighting faint and there was an eerie silence. She kept me waiting for three-quarters of an hour on a narrow, uncomfortable bench and when finally ushered into her presence I was expected to explain myself, although she knew perfectly well that I had come as John's publisher. I found it almost impossible to communicate with her, and, in spite of the fact that I had negotiated for months to make the appointment, I left after no more than ten minutes. I would have liked to have been able to share her mourning with her but she made it absolutely impossible.

LEN DEIGHTON

PUBLISHING LEN DEIGHTON is not simply to publish a terrific writer, it is to publish an extraordinary personality. Len's first book, *The Ipcress File*, was published by Hodder & Stoughton. He came to us with his second, *Horse Under Water*, and he told me the following story. Apparently the book jacket on all copies of *The Ipcress File* 'cockled', as he put it. Len was understandably disturbed by this and took it up with Hodder. They said it was because of the varnish. When you varnish a paper that is too light in weight, they explained, it may cockle. Len asked why they had not used a heavier paper. They said they would 'look into it'. He heard no more. The other, and even more serious, matter was that Hodder refused to tell Len how many copies they were printing. 'OK,' said Len, 'as long as you do not go out of print.' Meanwhile his agent, Jonathan Clowes, informed Hodder in his soft-spoken manner that he was hopeful of selling the serial rights. They were extremely sceptical. Then Jonathan rang to say he *had* sold the serial rights. To the *Evening Standard*. Hodder remained unimpressed. Not long thereafter Jonathan rang to say that Harry Salzman – 'You know,' he said, 'the producer of the James Bond films' – was seriously interested. And then Salzman bought the film rights. Even now Hodder remained unimpressed. The upshot of all this was that *The Ipcress File* went out of print within two weeks of publication and this is the reason why Len came to Cape.

Early on in our relationship I remember asking Len how he had hit upon the idea of his protagonist, Harry Palmer. His reply was that Ian Fleming's James Bond books had inspired him, giving him the idea of creating a character who was the exact opposite of James Bond. Len, of course, also found his own style and that too is the antithesis of Fleming's.

I have rarely had as much fun publishing an author. Len was demanding but that is his right. Meanwhile there were many delights. He shared my love of food but with one important distinction. He cooks and I don't. He frequently made his own ingredients. Certainly he would never offer pasta unless it was homemade. Even when cooking sausages he would make them himself: mince the meat, spice it, and feed the mix into a sausage skin. His kitchen in the Elephant and Castle was like a laboratory stacked with exotic ingredients. And there were always two or three pretty girls, usually models, acting as 'assistants', although they did little beyond adorning the place. In addition to his writing talents, Len was a gifted artist and he produced a weekly cookery strip (pictures and captions) for the *Observer*. We made a book of these and published them as *The Action Cookbook*. A cookbook unlike any other.

In negotiating the contract for *Horse Under Water* I had persuaded Jonathan Clowes to allow us – in this case me – to handle the serial rights, and I sold the book to the *Daily Express*. This was good going. Leading national newspapers are rarely interested in serializing a thriller. The *Daily Express* promotion was enormously effective and helped sell the book. I recall that they paid £3,000. When it came to the next book, *Funeral in Berlin*, the *Express* again offered £3,000 but Len felt we should ask for £4,000. I said, 'They won't pay it.' I had already tried. Len argued: 'They think they have a monopoly.'

I agreed that this was more or less the case. 'The only way we can deal with them', Len continued, 'is by not giving in.' So I didn't. They did not budge either and so there was no serial sale. For Len's subsequent book, he wanted me to ask for £5,000. The *Express* agreed and Len was over the moon. Of course the total earned came to less than if we had accepted their offer for *Funeral in Berlin*, but to Len, the principle was more important than the money. I enjoy his way of thinking.

When *Funeral in Berlin* was being filmed I flew with Len to Berlin. We spent an evening, plus much of a night, with Michael Caine, who was playing Harry Palmer in the film. Michael had heard about Berlin nightclubs apparently filled with the most gorgeous ladies, and so, after dinner, we set off to explore.

The first club we entered seemed, at a glance, to be the answer to our dreams. Michael put his arms around a fabulous

creature. As he did so her sleeve rose and he observed the hairs on her arm. She was a transvestite. We looked around the room and it was not difficult to see that this was applicable to all of them. We made a speedy exit and went on to the next club. Now we were wary and quick to see that these 'ladies' were more of the same. And so we continued from club to club to club. Michael was determined that the real thing must exist somewhere. It did not, or at least we did not find it. And so three drunken, disappointed Englishmen made their way through the streets of Berlin until the early hours of the morning.

A year or two later, Len bought a house in Albufeira, on the south coast of Portugal. He was one of the first foreigners to do so. The house was modest but its position was extraordinary. It stood very high on a cliff with its own steps (an enormous number of them) leading right down on to a deserted beach. Len invited me to stay for a few days and on my very first day I went straight down to the sea. Len announced he would remain in the house to do some painting. The following day he again seemed reluctant to accompany me. I asked whether he had a problem and he confessed, slightly ashamed of the fact, that he was unable to swim. He had tried many times but without success. I wondered if he would allow me to teach him. He was sceptical but I said I was an expert (a lie) and I coaxed him down. Teaching a grown man to swim is infinitely more difficult than teaching a child. But I am proud to report that by the time I left, five days later, Len was swimming. There remained a little work to be done on his breathing but I was impressed. And so was he.

An area in which Len excelled and the details of which did not especially interest Fleming was that of promotion. For example, one day Len brought one of his notebooks into the office. It was a work of art, created with a combination of Len's calligraphy and his detailed drawings. He suggested we might produce a facsimile of some pages and bind them up to send out as teasers to booksellers. An even more inspired idea was to reproduce a book of stamps. The outside was a facsimile of a normal stamp book and inside there were perforated stamps identical in size and colour to the real thing but with the head of Hitler in place of the face of the Queen. They sent shivers down one's spine.

It was frequently a joy to observe Len's mind at work. I will give one example – and this not related to a book. Len had decided to live in Ireland, which offered enormous tax advantages to writers. He is the least ostentatious of people and I cannot imagine him spending much money on himself, but the taxes payable in England by a writer as successful as he was stuck in his gullet. From Ireland he could easily visit London several times a year, and he kept a car there. Now, Len regarded the search for parking spaces as an irritating waste of time and so he parked his car regardless, which resulted in several tickets a day. These amounted to, say, £200 on a short stay. When he received his fine, Len sent a cheque for £500 and asked the authorities to kindly let him know when he owed further monies. They wrote back saying that it was £200 and not £500 he owed. They had no means of cashing what he had sent and so they returned his cheque. He wrote back deliberately misunderstanding and apologizing for his error, this time enclosing a cheque for £700 to cover the £200 plus the original £500. According to Len it was not long before they gave up on him.

One day I was having dinner with Len and the fashion photographer Duffy at the Trattoria Terrazza in Romilly Street. It was our favourite restaurant. Mario and Franco worked there then. Subsequently they went on to make a fortune. Alvaro also worked there, and decades later he still has his own restaurant called La Famiglia. We finished dinner at about 11 p.m. and Len took it into his head that it would be fun to drive to my cottage in the Black Mountains. All four of us (Len had a girl in tow). I pointed out that it would take three hours to get there. 'Not at night,' Len said. I really did not the least bit want to go and certainly not in such an unprepared way. But Len was determined and when he is determined he tends to get his way.

We arrived at my cottage at 2 a.m. Thank God, for once it was not raining and the car could get up the driveway. We consumed three bottles of wine and went to sleep. We woke late and were rewarded by a rare and glorious Welsh sunny day. There was nothing to eat for breakfast so we sat on the grass outside the cottage and then we drove back to London.

One day Jonathan Clowes rang me to say that Len had asked him to submit his next book to five publishers, including Cape. Len had received an enormous advance from America and apparently he wanted to find out what the book might command in England. I said to Jonathan, 'You know, any book by a successful author is bound to be worth more to a house that doesn't already publish the author than to one that does.' I went on: 'I think we have published Len extremely well and I would love to continue to do so. But if Len really wants a multiple submission then count me out.'

SOME AMERICAN WRITERS

IN THIS SECTION I will write briefly about five American authors. Two of them I nearly came to publish: Carson McCullers and Saul Bellow; one I took on from the very beginning of his career: Edward Albee; one came to us from another publishing house: Isaac Bashevis Singer; and finally, one was already with Cape when I joined: Irwin Shaw.

CARSON McCULLERS

On my New York trips the days were made up of visiting publishers and agents in more or less equal proportions. Then, of course, I would see as much of our authors as possible, but this was mainly in the evenings. Among the agents, although he was principally a theatrical agent, was Robbie Lantz. Because Robbie represented only a few writers, many publishers gave him a miss, and so he always seemed the more delighted to see me. He was very much to the point and on one occasion, just a few minutes after I had arrived, he asked straight out: 'How would you like to publish Carson McCullers?' 'Are you serious?' I replied.

It so happens that I had a passion for her work dating back to my late-teenage years. There was an almost supernatural quality about her writing which fascinated me. How did

Robbie know my feelings when we had never even mentioned her books? It is true that I had remarked on an extraordinary photograph that stood on Robbie's desk. This was a portrait of two crones, Carson McCullers and Isaak Dinesen, both of them ancient and witchlike. And in between them, filled with joy, her arms around their shoulders, was Marilyn Monroe. Robbie explained that he did not feel the Cresset Press were doing justice to Carson's work in England and that he thought I could do far better. In addition he had a hunch that Carson and I would get on well. So I must go to Nyack, where Carson lived. It is in New York State. There and back would take a day but I could not imagine a more rewarding way to spend my time. Robbie also confided in me that Carson had cancer but he added she was so strong that, skinny as she was, she would no doubt fight it off.

Carson opened the door to me and those enormous owl-like eyes stared as I entered. She coughed a great deal and also stuttered badly as a result of a recent stroke. All this, combined with her strong Southern accent, would be enough to make a normal person unintelligible. But strangely it was not the case with her. On my journey to Nyack I had wondered what we might talk about, but in the event this presented no problem at all. We chatted away like very old friends and I had to remind myself that I was in the presence of a great writer. In speaking of her new book (she did not tell me much) Carson said that progress was slow. I ventured to ask how many pages she had written and she stuttered, 'Seventeen.' I did not ask to read them for I knew that that was not what she wanted.

I visited Carson four more times on four more trips and then, before the fifth, she died. It is a cliché, but I shall never again meet anyone remotely like her.

SAUL BELLOW

A friend of mine told me that Saul Bellow was keen to change publishers. He was with Barley Allison but did not find being published by a tiny imprint within a bigger house (Secker & Warburg) satisfactory. I learned at the same time that Bellow was in London for just three days. It was the morning of day two, and you can imagine my excitement. This was long before Saul Bellow won the Nobel Prize but even then he was without question THE GREAT AMERICAN NOVELIST. Obviously I would put anything aside to have lunch with him. I rang right away and was fortunate to reach Bellow in his hotel. He knew who I was, which helped. I asked whether he might by chance be free for lunch that day or the next. The latter suited him well and so I made the arrangements, arriving at the restaurant at ten to one to find him already in place.

I mentioned one or two mutual friends, including Martin Amis (I happened to know that he was a fan of Martin's).

Bellow has a particularly low, soft-spoken voice, which complements his line in bitchery. He appears to delight in being malicious, a gentle smile accompanying his words. When we reached the main course I came to the point: 'I hear you are thinking of moving. Is that so?' He nodded. Inevitably I made a case for Cape. I said that *Herzog* was one of the greatest contemporary novels. It was the truth, but of course he liked to hear it, and we indulged in some publishing talk. Then Bellow announced that he would like to be published by Cape. There was no doubt about what he had said and I just left it in the air so to speak. I planned to write to him. This I did the following day and he wrote back confirming his wish. I read and re-read his letter. I took a childish pride in it. And then he went silent. I felt I could neither pursue him nor reproach him. It had been too good to be true. All this was many years ago but even now I cannot help feeling that he owes me an explanation.

EDWARD ALBEE

I was on my second trip to the States when I heard about two plays by a young playwright that were running in a tiny theatre in Greenwich Village. The playwright was called Edward Albee and the plays were *The Zoo Story* and *The Death of Bessie Smith*. It sounded like an evening I would enjoy.

The plays impressed me enormously, so much so that I got in touch with Albee's agent. Not surprisingly the British publishing rights were free and I bought them for a tiny advance. I recall running into André Deutsch in the bar at the Algonquin, where we were both staying. (The hotel is famous for the fact that James Thurber and the whole *New Yorker* gang used to meet there daily.) André, in his competitive way, asked whether I had bought anything. I told him about the plays and he said, 'You are mad.' I was not surprised that he should think so.

I had heard that Albee was exceptionally shy and so I did not seek him out. We continued to publish him for many years and I was lucky in that the plays I had seen were followed almost immediately by *Who's Afraid of Virginia Woolf?*. This was an enormous hit all over the world and it was later made into a film starring Richard Burton and Elizabeth Taylor. Before long Albee was hailed as the greatest American playwright since Arthur Miller. Apart from *Virginia Woolf* we never sold many copies of his plays. Nevertheless it was satisfying to publish him, though it always seemed to me regrettable that there should be no contact between us.

Then, one summer, I was in Long Island visiting a number of my authors when someone mentioned that they had just spent an evening with Albee. He lived, it seemed, in East Hampton and now I found myself moved to visit him. And so I rang. The voice on the other end of the line was not exactly welcoming but I persisted. I was round the corner and my desire to drop in seemed perfectly reasonable. Within a few minutes of my arrival at his house Albee made me feel uncomfortable. It was clear that the intrusion was unwelcome and I left.

ISAAC BASHEVIS SINGER

Over lunch in New York the publisher Roger Straus said to me: 'I think I must move Isaac Bashevis Singer. The Secker performance is pathetic. I'll bet you could do better.' I had only read two Singer books, enough to realize he clearly had a voice of his own and a deeply touching one. In addition he was a remarkable storyteller. Singer was still writing in Yiddish but the translations were so good that you would not know it. I was more than interested: I was really keen. The only condition Roger made (I got the impression that Singer did not have a great deal to say in the matter) was that we should be willing to republish the backlist. We made a deal and I greatly looked forward to meeting the old boy on my next New York trip. It so happened that Regina would be accompanying me, which seemed especially appropriate since (though born in New York) she speaks Polish and Russian.

I rang Singer two days after our arrival and invited him and his wife to dinner. He insisted that he take us. No question about it. He proposed that we come to his apartment at 6 p.m. (Not a good sign!) And from there we would go to his favourite restaurant around the corner. The apartment, high on the West Side, was dark, dingy and dusty. Books were piled almost to the ceiling against every wall and alongside the books were piles of old newspapers. Singer addressed only me. Regina was not only unable to show off her languages but was hardly permitted to speak a word. The same applied to Singer's wife. By now it was 7 p.m. and the time had come to go to the restaurant. I feared the worst. It was worse than the worst. We were heading for a place that served only the most basic fare, with nothing to drink except water and apple juice.

By way of the greatest possible contrast, the next time I saw Singer was in Stockholm. There in the grand hall stood this diminutive figure poised to collect the Nobel Prize for Literature, the highest literary award in the world. I felt immensely proud of him and could not imagine what he would do with so much money. But I am willing to bet that he and Alma continued to go regularly to the restaurant around the corner.

IRWIN SHAW

You may recall there was one important American writer already present on the Cape list when I joined. It was Irwin Shaw, author of *The Young Lions*.

This brings us to Klosters, where Irwin and his wife Marion owned a chalet. Their house was full (as the chalets of those living in ski resorts tend to be) and so I booked into the Weineck. It is not an unfashionable hotel and costs a quarter of the highly desirable Grischuna Hotel.

On my first night I was invited to the Shaws for dinner. Among the guests was Deborah Kerr with her husband Peter Viertel. Deborah was still extremely beautiful and Peter a tall, handsome man who had written a novel in his twenties called *White Hunter, Black Heart*. (The book became well known and caught the attention of Ernest Hemingway, who took a shine to Peter and invited him to join various hunting expeditions.) Peter was the son of Berthold Viertel. His father ran the Burg Theater, the leading theatre in Vienna, and Berthold happened to be a friend of my father's. In this fashionable scene, an element of special interest to my mind is the fact that Peter's mother, Tsalka, was Greta Garbo's best friend. Garbo, alas, was not present during my stay but she was apparently a frequent visitor.

After dinner, Irwin asked if I would like to join him and a couple of friends skiing the following morning. This involved a helicopter flight to one of the surrounding mountains. They never skied the famous Passen Run nor did they stoop to any other piste skiing. The snow was simply not good enough and then there were the crowds. With the help of a helicopter they could ski exclusively in virgin snow. Irwin went on to mention that the cost was most reasonable. A mere $500, which would of course be divided by four. It may have been reasonable to him, but it was too much for me.

The purpose of my stay was to show an interest in Irwin's work and also to talk to him about a book of stories on which he was working and some of which I had read. I had a hunch that it might not be easy to arrange a quiet moment with Irwin and so I thought I'd take a stab at it without delay. As I left I suggested a drink at the Grischuna for the following evening, which Irwin seemed to welcome. I arrived some fifteen minutes prior to the appointed hour of 7 p.m. While I sat sipping my Martini three or four people came into the bar, two of whom I recognized from Irwin's dinner. When Irwin turned up half an hour late at 7.30 p.m. he brought a small gang with him. So much for our quiet chat. To make amends, Irwin suggested that we meet quietly at 7 p.m. the following day at his chalet. When I got there I found a cocktail party in full swing. It became clear to me that Irwin likes to be surrounded at all times and so I gave up my efforts to meet him privately.

On night three I was invited to dinner by Deborah and Peter. I was thrilled to be in their chalet above Klosters. They had built it many years previously and the house represents a dream of a movie-star home, far, far away from Hollywood. It was furnished with exquisite Swiss antiques and had the most magnificent fireplace along one wall of the drawing room. Some of the guests were again those I had met previously with Irwin. A new face was a man called Fred Chandon, whom I liked immediately. On my way home from dinner I spotted a very beautiful woman wearing enormous snow boots. She held the arm of her husband, Romain Gary, the French novelist and Prix Goncourt winner. It was Jean Seberg walking through the night to the Grischuna. The following day I left for London.

Later I heard that Marion and Irwin's marriage had broken up and then a couple of years after that I heard that they had run into each other in New York on Fifth Avenue. They fell into each other's arms and got together again.

DESMOND MORRIS

WHEN I MET Desmond Morris he was curator of mammals at London Zoo, a position he had held for many years. He lived just next to the Zoo, off Regent's Park Road, whilst I lived in Chalcot Crescent, about five minutes' walk from him. We were at a party given by mutual friends and I spotted Desmond immediately. Although he had a bland, roundish face there was something striking about him. Atop the face were strands of hair which he stroked frequently to put them into place. He spoke with enormous energy and rarely made a statement lacking in originality. On this occasion he was talking about ethology – the study of the behaviour of animals in their natural environment. His special interest lay in what humans might learn from other mammals. At the Zoo, he was ideally placed for such a study. Desmond was surrounded by a group of people who were obviously as intrigued by him as I was. One felt he was accustomed to being the centre of attention. While holding forth he referred casually to 'the Naked Ape', using the phrase simply to make a conversational point. For me, there was something poignant, almost magical, about those words. It may sound premature, but even at this first meeting I found myself suggesting to Desmond that *The Naked Ape* would make a superb title for a book. It was a book, naturally, that I felt Desmond should contemplate writing.

At the time, Desmond fronted a Granada television programme called *Zoo Time*. (One of our young authors, Sheena McKay, once told me that she had kissed the screen whenever he appeared.) This is an indication of the star that he was. While Desmond found television extremely well paid, his experience with publishing had been anything but happy from a financial point of view. Not one of his books – *Men and Snakes, Men and Apes, Men and Pandas* – had sold more than 4,000 copies, and now he found himself faced by a fanatic who talked in terms of hundreds of thousands, even millions, of copies of an as yet unwritten book. However, if the book were as successful as I anticipated, Desmond feared that he would lose credibility in serious scientific circles. For a scientist to write a 'popular' book (and, God forbid, one that earns millions of pounds) constitutes an unforgivable sin.

Over a three-year period I had lunch with Desmond many times. I made a point of underlining my confidence in the book by proposing that he name his own advance. Finally he agreed to a contract. I suggested that he should choose any sum from £1,000 to £10,000. He chose £3,000. A few days after he had committed himself I went round to his house and together we worked on a chapter breakdown. We achieved this in half a day. By then we had talked over the material so many times that the structure came easily. Desmond declared that he would write the book in what he called 'white heat'. He would begin in the afternoon each day and work through the night until 7 a.m. The only interruptions were to be the odd raid of his refrigerator. His estimate of the writing time was three months and this turned out to be exact. I remember how the day he finished he was so excited he brought the manuscript round to my house, and I in turn was so excited that I pushed everything else aside and read it immediately. It was a Sunday, and I was impatient to share my experience with colleagues at the office, but that had to wait until the following day.

At Cape we were unanimous. This was a book that would enthral and inform an enormous number of readers. We began to send out copies of the manuscript to foreign publishers and the response was such that it was immediately clear the book would be an international event, not only from the size of the advances offered, but also from the fact that the translation rights were not simply being bought by the main countries (Germany, France and Italy), but also by those more obscure in publishing terms, such as Greece, Israel and even Iceland.

Another heartening factor was the interest in serial rights. It wasn't just that we were able to sell the rights to a newspaper (unusual for this kind of book) but that we received a number of competing offers. We chose the *Sunday Mirror* in preference to the *Sunday Times*, who were equally eager, because we felt that the *Mirror* would increase book sales more than a 'classy' paper. Just as we had predicted, the staggering success of *The Naked Ape* did Desmond's scientific reputation nothing but harm. He became a considerable celebrity. Even I found myself praised. At a Hatchard's Authors of the Year party the fabled Billy (William) Collins came up to me and said simply: 'Congratulations.' I had no idea what he was talking about and asked him what he meant. He replied: 'On the way you have published *The Naked Ape*.' It was not long before the title found its way into the *Oxford Dictionary*.

Desmond's commercial success notwithstanding, there was an unexpected bonus. It took the form of a long and immensely complimentary letter from the Nobel Laureate Nico Tinbergen, who expressed his gratitude to Desmond for having contributed in a significant way to science by making ethology a subject of concern to the general public.

The financial gains of *The Naked Ape* resulted in Desmond's decision to take up residence in Malta. There were tax advantages of course, but in addition Malta has the asset of being a sunny place with no language barrier for the English. Desmond is not much of a linguist and so he found Malta particularly attractive. He bought a grand villa with a large lemon grove and he imported a full-size billiard table and a Rolls Royce to accompany it. The only other Rolls Royce in Malta belonged to the Governor – a fact that constantly amused Desmond. When I visited him, I pleaded that we should not drive in the Rolls, which could barely pass through the narrow lanes. I much preferred the sports car that belonged to Desmond's wife, Ramona. The danger to pedestrians apart, the act of sitting in a Rolls in such an impoverished country made me feel uncomfortable. Desmond is not normally ostentatious and I found this car business strangely uncharacteristic.

Another aspect of his life in Malta which bemused me was that we were subjected, daily, to a three-course hot lunch. His rationale for this ordeal in the heat was that the servants lived too far from the villa to be able to return to their homes after cooking an evening meal. Oh, how the rich punish themselves! Occasionally Desmond and I would go out to dinner in a restaurant, leaving Ramona at home. She was bringing up her baby in best chimp fashion – that is to say, with maximum body contact – and so she hardly ever left the house.

One of my greatest delights in Malta was to visit Valletta together with Desmond and sit at a pavement café indulging in an activity for which he coined the name 'manwatching'. I suggested that the subject (and the title also) would make a wonderful book, and with that our partnership went into action again. The book was ultimately published in a large format and very lavishly illustrated. It became Desmond's second most successful title.

From there Desmond went on to write an impressive number of other books and he also returned to an early passion, painting. (While still in his twenties he shared a show with Miró, no less.) To my pride and joy Desmond gave me two of his early paintings. Now he has a modern gallery to himself (the Major Gallery), and an enormous artbook reproducing his work has been published.

The quest for another book as original and as special as *The Naked Ape* eluded us. We talked of it on dozens of occasions over the years. Sometimes we seemed to be getting close, but it did not come about. I think as a publisher I have identified with Desmond more intimately than with any other author. Certainly my contribution to his career has been exceptional, and I have enjoyed his company for decades with never a cross word. He has come to my house for dinner on literally hundreds of occasions, sometimes with others and frequently alone. I had thought that we were the closest of friends. And then I felt there was a cooling. It was inexplicable. I was so sure of our relationship that I wrote to Desmond attempting to explore what had happened. He claimed not to have any idea what I was talking about. This is difficult to believe. It is now more than ten years since I have heard from Desmond. I console myself that in publishing friendship is often at risk.

THE BOOKER PRIZE

VERY MANY YEARS AGO, in the fifties, I was invited by the Society of Young Publishers to give a talk. The subject I chose was literary prizes since I felt passionately about them and hardly anyone in the literary world seemed to care. So, in my talk, I emphasized what I considered to be the importance of such prizes. Around the world (in America, Italy, Germany, Spain, and especially in France) this importance has been recognized. In England the most highly esteemed prize at the time was the Somerset Maugham Award. It was worth £250 and that was to be used for travel purposes. The winning book might sell an additional 500 copies, but no more. I went on to talk lyrically of my youthful experiences in Paris, at a time when the prizes were invariably announced in the autumn, and everyone I knew shared in a frenzy of excitement. Then, as now, there was not just one prize but many, the most important of which was the Prix Goncourt. In this case the winner could sell as many as 500,000 copies of a book which otherwise might have had a very modest sale of a mere 5,000 copies. Within a week of the prize announcement most of the people I saw would have read the book and it would have become the subject of discussion. In England, I said, it was unlikely that we could replicate the effect of the Goncourt but at least we could take inspiration from it.

The audience seemed excited at the prospect, and then

someone said, 'That's all very well, but where will the money for the prize come from?' I had a notion and I undertook to try. The company I thought of approaching was Booker Brothers. They were rich and were involved, among other enterprises, in the farming of sugar cane in the West Indies. I went to see Charles Tyrell at Booker and asked whether they would be willing to put a relatively small sum of money into a literary prize for fiction. I should add that the reason I thought especially of Booker was that they had formed a company to purchase literary copyrights in partnership with certain very successful authors, notably Agatha Christie and Ian Fleming. This entailed tax advantages for the author and resulted in considerable profits for Booker. It so happened that we were Ian Fleming's publishers and that is how I had some knowledge of the degree to which their venture had been profitable. Within a few days Tyrell came back to me with a yes. And that is how the Booker Prize came about.

Now that we had a prize, we began to discuss details from an organizational point of view. I suggested we call upon the National Book League to administer it. The head of this organization was Martyn Goff and he has brilliantly championed the prize from that day to this. We agreed that we wanted five judges (one of them to be a Chair) and that we would set up a committee to choose these judges. We also agreed that only British and Commonwealth writers should be eligible. To begin with the prize money was £5,000 and we decided to have a drinks event at the Guildhall for the announcement. I think my most worthwhile suggestion was that we should each year announce a shortlist of six, from which the winner would be chosen. It seemed to me most desirable that there should be as much speculation as possible prior to the final announcement. Having a shortlist would also mean that six authors benefited rather than just one. There were to be three judging sessions and at the third, a month before the Day, both shortlist and winner would be selected, although the name of the winner was to be kept a closely guarded secret.

So far so good. Alas, on several occasions the name of the winner was leaked. One year, a judge went so far as to write an account of the judging sessions and, believe it or not, he named the winner a month ahead of time. After some years we decided that there was only one guarantee of secrecy and that was for the judges to make the choice of the winner immediately before the lavish sit-down dinner which by that time had replaced the drinks event. From a secrecy point of view the last-minute decision was clearly essential. From a human point of view it has its drawbacks, for the contenders are under an enormous strain as they sit dining and waiting for the announcement.

The first year of the Booker Prize was 1969. The winner was *Something to Answer For* by P. H. Newby. The book got on to the *Evening Standard* bestseller list where it stayed for a few weeks. That was the first time a novel published in England had appeared on a bestseller list as a result of winning a literary award. The novel sold an additional 3,000 copies – not many, but we were triumphant. We knew that we were on the way. The prize began to be televised early in its life. It also began to be given substantial space in the press. The turning point for the Booker came in 1980. That year two heavyweights were in competition and this resulted in a great deal of speculation. The books in question were *Rites of Passage* by William Golding and *Earthly Powers* by Anthony Burgess. Golding won but if it had been Burgess the effect on sales would have been equally great. I do not entirely trust the figures from some publishers but I can say from my own experience that when Anita Brookner won with *Hotel du Lac* in 1984 we sold 80,000 copies. Prior to that we had never sold more than 7,000 copies of any of Anita's books.

The Booker has on more than one occasion suffered a

setback. This was the case in 1972, when John Berger won with his novel *G*. In those days the dinner was given at the Café Royal and it was there that Berger got up to make his acceptance speech. He announced that he would give half his prize money to the Black Panther Movement. This was in protest at what he called Booker's 'colonialist policies', i.e. their sugar plantations. I wonder why Berger did not either decline the prize altogether or give *all* the money to the Black Panthers. Another controversy occurred two years later, in 1974, when the entries included Kingsley Amis's *Ending Up*. Elizabeth Jane Howard was one of the judges and married to Amis. At the shortlist meeting she announced: 'I had better leave the room, it is easily Kingsley's best book. It is a masterpiece, but I must not influence you.' I do not know what she thought she was doing as a judge.

Now the prize has become by far the biggest event in the literary calendar. Regardless of who wins, it always commands enormous attention. A television programme is guaranteed and several channels even vie for the right to cover the prize. At the time of the announcement of the shortlist an enormous amount of media space is devoted to it. Strange as it may sound, when I look back on my publishing life I think the Booker Prize may well be my most useful and lasting contribution.

ROALD DAHL

THIS IS HOW I met Roald Dahl. His children's books were published by Rayner Unwin of Allen and Unwin, but Dahl came to feel he wanted to be with what he termed a 'proper' children's book publisher and asked his agent to set up five interviews. One of them was with me. To my great surprise he decided in favour of Cape, something I found all the more flattering since self-evidently I was far from the expert he had sought.

The first book of Roald's we published was *Danny the Champion of the World*, in 1975. Roald wanted Jill Bennett to illustrate the book. She had illustrated his other novels for children. Jill Bennett is a strictly realistic artist, and whilst she is good in her way I found her work unimaginative. Cautiously I questioned his choice. Roald explained that he thought illustrations should do no more than simply complement the text. His personality was formidable, especially to someone new to it, and so I shut up. When it came to *The Enormous Crocodile*, Roald's next book, in 1978, I knew him rather better and suggested he at least consider a different illustrator. This time I was at a slight advantage in that the notion of the book was mine. Ever since Roald had joined Cape I had tried to persuade him to write a text for a picture book, an idea he'd always countered by pointing out that although such a book would involve relatively few pages of text it would be even more difficult to write than a novel. When Roald finally succumbed and wrote *The Enormous Crocodile* (incidentally the text was rather on the long side) I managed to persuade him that Quentin Blake would make the perfect artist. I proposed that I would collect samples of the work of various artists so that Roald could come in to my office to consider what was on offer.

Some of the artists I selected were published by Cape, others elsewhere, but of all of them, the one I favoured was Quentin Blake. Roald, on the other hand, thought his work too idiosyncratic. Still determined, I gave him three of Quentin's books to take home, in the hope that he might come round to my way of thinking. He rang a few days later and said, 'Your chap is really good, you know.' And that was that, not only for *The Enormous Crocodile* but for the rest of Roald's life. As their partnership progressed, Roald became more and more enamoured of Quentin's work, until I felt he had not only overcome his reservations but totally forgotten them. With each book he was delighted anew at the manner in which Quentin had caught the essence of the characters so precisely.

When Roald won the Whitbread Prize for *Matilda*, as the best children's book of the year, I recall saying to him in the taxi on the way to the brewery for the presentation that it must be a bit of a bore to attend such a function. 'Not at all,' he said. 'You may not realize it, but this is the first award I have ever received.' I had not realized this and to me it is a reflection of an astonishing neglect. I speak of the degree to which the experts underrate Roald. He has never been dismissed but somehow he is disapproved of. I have frequently known such a thing to happen to enormously successful and also wealthy writers, but in Roald's case I feel there is a profound and inexplicable underestimation of the quality of his work, which I would call genius.

As I got to know Roald better over the years, I gradually became a part of his extended family. He made being in his company the most pleasurable of experiences. It was a delight to visit him at Gypsy House, in Great Missenden. There, some fifty yards from the main house, stood Roald's hut, where he wrote all his books, sitting in a shabby armchair. Between them, Roald and the chair took up more than half the space. The place looked a terrible mess but the few relics Roald had scattered about gave it an extraordinarily powerful flavour. The flavour of Roald's personality.

When I came to dinner Roald would invariably offer me a special bottle or two from his excellent cellar. He did not simply buy good wine, he understood it. Frequently he and his wife Liccy would invite me to stay the night. On such occasions we played billiards, a game he loved. I was no good at all and he always won easily. Over the course of these visits to Gypsy House I had the pleasure of getting to know and admire Liccy, the love of Roald's life. As I had learned early on, his marriage to the actress Patricia Neill was long over. It was a joy to observe how much Liccy loved and cared for him. They adored each other.

Among Roald's many qualities was great generosity. I experienced this in a most unusual way. A decade ago I suffered for several months from a serious depression, as the result of which I was unable to concentrate on anything, and my doctor advised me to take time off. I chose to live in the South of France, and there I received from Roald the longest and the most wonderful letter of my life. The letter was in longhand (nine closely written pages) and must have taken Roald several days to write. He was doing so simply to cheer me on. And he succeeded in a very big way.

Thoughtful and kind as Roald could be, he would on occasion get very angry, especially if he felt slighted, or worse, cheated. This was, for example, the case with his American publishers. I never mastered all the details, but I know that money was involved and it made Roald feel bitter. So bitter that he not only left the publishers but for the rest of his life never forgave them.

When it came to Roald's seventieth birthday we naturally wanted to give a special dinner for him. We chose the Garrick Club as the venue. I asked Roald if there was anyone he would especially like us to invite and he came up with two names. The first was Joanna Lumley, because she was so attractive and intelligent. She was delighted to accept. The second was a more problematical choice. It was Francis Bacon. I do not recall whether they had ever met but Roald admired Bacon's work greatly and had bought two of his paintings many years previously. The problem lay in the fact that Bacon had a reputation of behaving in an unruly and drunken manner. I was determined to 'deliver' Bacon for Roald although the odds seemed to me heavily against his accepting an invitation to a formal event. And even if he did accept there was the danger of his arriving in such a state that the Garrick would refuse him entry. As it turned out, Bacon accepted promptly and in writing. On the day he put everyone to shame by wearing a dark blue pinstripe suit, a white shirt and a tie. He was by far the most immaculately dressed man at the table. And, as if that were not enough, he was consistently entertaining and urbane. He made an enormous contribution to the success of the evening. As he left, he said goodbye most graciously and thanked me for asking him. I saw him out to the door and watched as he headed off towards nearby Soho. I could not help wondering what the rest of the night might hold in store for him.

In his last years Roald suffered from leukaemia. He was obviously in great pain much of the time. One could constantly see it on his face and yet I never heard him complain. When he died Liccy determined to carry on his charity work. She created the Roald Dahl Foundation in his memory and beyond that she has raised money for a Roald Dahl museum to be built in Great Missenden. She has virtually dedicated her life to these projects.

Not long after Roald's death I had the idea of editing a book to be called *The Roald Dahl Treasury*, an anthology of extracts from his books. It would be a big book of 448 pages and very lavishly illustrated. Many of the illustrations were by Quentin Blake but I also invited the participation of a number of artists who had not previously illustrated Roald. While working on *The Treasury*, the notion of an auction occurred to me. I approached a friend, Melanie Clore, who is the deputy chairman of Sotheby's, and proposed to her (assuming I could persuade the artists in question to donate the proceeds of their work) that Sotheby's hold an auction of the pictures in the book. They would take no share and all the money would go to one of Roald's favourite charities. Every one of the artists agreed and we were off. The fact that this was an art event, given Roald's passion for collecting pictures, made it particularly poignant. The auction proved a triumph and some of the illustrations were sold for two, three or four times the price anticipated. The occasion was exceptionally joyful for everyone present. It was also of course an excellent way to promote the book. I know that Roald would have approved.

PUBLISHING CHILDREN'S BOOKS

AT THE TIME I joined Cape in 1960, we had a very small children's book list. It included a few important novelists – Arthur Ransome, Hugh Lofting (the Dr Dolittle books), Joan Aiken and Erich Kästner, author of *Emil and the Detectives*, who had also been published by my father in his small publishing house in Berlin. My father was immensely proud of publishing Kästner.

I was totally ignorant of publishing books for children. By pure chance a lady called Ann Carter, who read and reported on adult books for us, mentioned to me that a friend of hers who lived in a studio in Percy Street, around the corner from my office, had produced a wonderful picture book. Apparently he had hawked it round a number of publishers but without success. Ann proposed that I might take a look at his work and I did so, really just to please her. So I went to visit the artist, John Burningham.

For an artist in search of a publisher John struck me as surprisingly surly, although he melted at my effusive praise. His book, called *Borka*, was a story of a goose born without feathers. There was one picture that impressed me especially, which depicted the mother goose knitting a new wing for her child, with total concentration. At her feet we see the little fellow poised eagerly, waiting. I explained my lack of expertise but undertook to champion the book, at which point John

allowed me to carry away to my office the large cardboard folder which held his illustrations. There my boss, Bob Wren Howard, co-founder of the company together with the recently deceased Jonathan Cape, thought me quite deranged. He explained patiently that in the case of a colour book, production costs would be so high that, prior to contracting, one had to put together something called a co-edition (that is, find foreign publishers ready to join the printing). My enthusiasm for *Borka* was so great that I pleaded the case for going ahead regardless. Wren Howard remained unconvinced and yet he agreed, a vote of confidence for which I felt most grateful. I must add that he was soon to be rewarded. By the day of publication we had sold *Borka* in eight countries and the book went on to win the Kate Greenaway Medal, awarded by the Library Association for the best children's picture book of the year. This award normally goes to an artist with a body of work and had never before been given for a first book. John was twenty-nine at the time.

I went on to publish some thirty books by John, who has long been recognized as one of the most talented British artists. His most perfect book, in my opinion, is *Mr Gumpy's Outing*, and this also won the Kate Greenaway award. Some years later he produced *Grandpa*. It is a simple story of the relationship between a little girl and her grandfather. For the last page John drew a picture of an empty armchair. Grandpa is dead. This poignant book shows markedly his extraordinary ability to move a child. Indeed, to move an adult also. I was so excited by the book that within an hour of John bringing it in to me, I decided to telephone John Coates, the producer of the wonderful animated film of *The Snowman* by Raymond Briggs. To my delight I reached Coates immediately and to my even greater delight it turned out that his office was in Charlotte Street, around the corner from where John lived, and also very near my office. I told John Coates, whom I had never met before, that I had just received a book which I had a hunch he might want to film. How soon could he come to look at it, I asked. He said he could manage later that afternoon. When he saw the book he said, 'I think you are right.' The moment he left I rang John to share the news with him. So often, of course, things go wrong in the film world, but in this case Coates made the film. Not only that, but it was true to the book.

After the triumphant success of *Borka* I inevitably wanted to try to repeat it. All we needed was another artist of comparable quality. I began to look out for such a person. It was at this point that I decided to take on the role of Children's Book Editor in addition to my adult publishing. I had a lot to learn but ultimately I have found publishing children's books every bit as satisfying as my work for adults and I cannot think of another adult publisher who has embraced the same challenge.

My dream was realized with the work of Quentin Blake. The first of his own (text and pictures) books that we published was *Patrick*, in 1969. We have continued to publish Quentin ever since and he has written the texts for almost all his picture books. He is the most literate of the artists I know and has a natural gift for writing. But of course by far his most important talent is as illustrator, with his unique style which is much loved by children and also by adults. Quentin's imagination is boundless. I have had the pleasure of publishing him for

close to forty years and he has never ceased to delight me.
Two of my favourite books are *Clown* (a book without
words) and *Zagazoo*. We have always worked harmoniously
together and Quentin seems to welcome whatever critical
contribution I am able to make. I can think of many artists
very much less talented and also less successful than Quentin
who take criticism a lot less kindly. For many years Quentin
taught illustration at the Royal College of Art and then he held
a professorship there.

Of course my greatest contribution was to 'marry' him to
Roald Dahl, a story I have told in the previous section. The
collaboration with Roald Dahl was very much between the
two of them and I was no more than an onlooker. But when
Cape came to publish *The Roald Dahl Treasury* I had the joy
of working intimately with Quentin. We met once a week and
planned every aspect of the book together. Each week Quentin
brought in his new drawings and it was tremendously exciting
to see the work develop. Then one day, which I shall not
forget, Quentin came in and said, 'What are we going to do
next?' Clearly he had enjoyed our working together as much
as I did and would miss it equally.

In 1999 Quentin was chosen to be our first Children's
Laureate. The idea stemmed originally from the Poet Laureate, Ted Hughes, and Michael Morpurgo. The object was to
promote the importance of children's books. For a two-year

period Quentin put all his energy into the task. He did a magnificent job but was so selfless that inevitably he seriously neglected his own work.

I take a particular delight in the fact that all the artists we published (I mean every one of them) work in a style totally different from one another. At the risk of sounding grandiose I should add that they are also different from artists published by anyone else. The only explanation I can offer is that the quality for which I look above all is that an artist should work directly from the heart. Like other publishers, I see portfolios by new artists. Sometimes I am shown a few pictures and then the artist says, 'I can work in this other style also.' At that point I know that the work is not for me.

We come to the work of Nicola Bayley. I saw three pieces of hers on show at the Royal College of Art. (These became part of a book we subsequently published as *One Old Oxford Ox*.) They were Nicola's final work as a student at the College and I thought them inordinately beautiful, close to perfect. I was immediately convinced that Nicola would be a star and that we should publish her. I wanted to offer her a contract right away, but I had no suitable text and so I proposed a book of nursery rhymes. Nicola was enchanted by the idea and this became her first book. When it was finished, I decided that we should call it *Nicola Bayley's Book of Nursery Rhymes*. Even today I am proud of the bravado of this; my conviction that the book would make her famous was so strong that putting her name in the title did not seem at all outlandish.

At the time of publication, I arranged for the *Sunday Times* to do a big feature on Nicola's work and readers were invited to send in children's stories she might illustrate. This seemed a good idea but of the 10,000 entries we received not a single one turned out to be suitable. Worse, we had stupidly failed to say that entrants must state the nature of the submission on the envelope and this resulted in chaos. For a period of two weeks or so it took several days to sort out the letters and for any of us to receive our 'normal' post.

The story of our relationship with Nicola Bayley does not end happily, however. Our overseas representative at the time was a man called Sebastian Walker, a friend of mine, or so I thought. When Sebastian started his own company (Walker Books) he is reputed to have taken a suitcase full of money round to Nicola and subsequently persuaded her to join him at Walker. I never spoke to Sebastian again. Nor, for that matter, did I speak again to Nicola. Fully to explain my anger against Walker, I should say that when he announced his first twelve artists and writers, the majority were from Cape.

I came to feel a real measure of confidence in myself as a publisher of picture books. The judgement of artwork, compared with that of writing, seemed to me remarkably simple. The aspect of publishing picture books I found especially satisfying was that of matching artist to writer. When I first read Russell Hoban's story *Captain Najork*, I immediately thought of Quentin Blake as illustrator, and this resulted in one of the finest picture books (combining text and pictures) of recent decades.

Speaking of text and pictures leads me to mention a prize founded by my late father, called the Kurt Maschler Prize. My father had found the perfect illustrator for Erich Kästner's work in Walter Trier. And it was this relationship that inspired him to found his prize, which is given for the best combination of illustration and text in a picture book. The winner receives a bronze 'Emil' replica of Trier's drawing, plus a cheque for £1,000.

One obvious source of artists is art schools, and another is agents. However, an avenue I have found particularly rewarding is to approach an artist I admire in a related field. This was the case with Posy Simmonds. Her marvellous strip in the *Guardian* inspired me to imagine that she might produce equally wonderful children's books. I put the idea to her and it resulted in her first book, *Fred*, followed by several equally original and delightful children's books.

On other occasions, the genesis of a picture book may be a specific idea in the mind of a publisher. I will give just one particularly successful example. My idea was to publish an explicit (and preferably also entertaining book) that would explain to the really young (from two upwards) how babies are made. I had something of a missionary zeal about this idea, having never understood the desire of educationalists, and for that matter parents, to make a secret of this all-important subject.

My first choice was the artist Babette Cole because I felt confident of her style, her humour, her imagination – in short, her perfect ability to take on the project. I was not her publisher but I did not hesitate to approach her. She loved the subject and said she would like to take it on. She immediately invented the perfect title, *Mummy Laid an Egg*, and we were off to a brilliant start. Babette's genius was to find a structure through which the story could be told without vulgarity. She decided to begin the book with parents offering the usual idiotic coy explanations where, for example, it is the stork who brings the baby, or the baby is hatched from an egg. Then, after such nonsense, the children take over in the book. 'No, it's none of that,' they say. And they go on to tell their parents what really happens, including a description of 'the act' itself.

I should add that a large number of publishers turned out to be great puritans. The worst were the Americans: a total of twenty-one American publishers declined the book.

After *Mummy Laid an Egg* I proposed to Babette that we think of it as the first in a series of books for children on taboo subjects. Among the titles we have published are *Two of Everything* (divorce) and *Hair in Funny Places* (puberty).

Babette welcomes an unusually active contribution from her publisher and this makes working with her a particular delight.

Finally, we come to a man I would call a genius. He is Roberto Innocenti, an Italian from Florence, and I was introduced to his work through his first book, *Rose Blanche*. I saw a copy at the annual Bologna Book Fair, the leading international children's book fair. Its subject was the war, children and concentration camps. I greatly admired the pictures but initially and regretfully turned the book down, as I thought the subject matter made it impossible to sell in England. The publisher offering the rights told me several other publishers had said Cape would be by far the best bet. I could see the book's importance but stood my ground. I said, 'Why don't you try four other publishers, and if they all decline please feel free to come back to me.' They did, and so did the publisher, at which point I bought the rights. We went into five printings and sold over 20,000 copies.

The more I looked at the book, the more I admired it, and I was determined to talk to Innocenti about taking on another subject. We met and I asked him whether he had any ideas. He said he had only one dream and that was to illustrate *Pinocchio*. (The story, as everyone knows, was immortalized by Disney, but the original was by an Italian, Colado.) What I had in mind was a thirty-two-page picture book comparable in length to *Rose Blanche*, but what the artist was proposing was a 200-page book! All in colour. I was so in love with Innocenti's work that I agreed to commission him. By the following year he had produced enough pictures for me to offer the project to foreign publishers at Bologna. Not just to 'offer' it but to sell it around the world. Everybody agreed that the pictures were magnificent and our stand was besieged as I have never seen it before or since. At Bologna publishers often talk of 'the Book of the Fair'. That year it was *Pinocchio*.

I have mentioned the city of Bologna but I must convey in

a few words how very special it is. Wherever you walk you will encounter architectural beauty, and because there is no Leonardo da Vinci, no Michelangelo, Bologna is relatively free of tourists. It is a privilege simply to be there. To cross the Piazza Maggiore in the morning or to cross it lit up at night is a rare joy. It is enough to drive you crazy and it did just that to a group of us one evening – John Burningham, Ian Craig, Rolf Inhauser and myself. We were on our way back from dinner when in the middle of the square, we came upon a dented Coca-Cola tin. We began to play football with it, using

our jackets as goalposts. We were off. Within a few minutes some twenty publishers, artists and people from Bologna had joined us and taken sides. For a while we felt as carefree and joyous as children. Then we saw lights blazing. The entire square was surrounded by Italian police cars: we had been soiling the sacred square. We duly apologized and disbanded. It had been a glorious quarter of an hour, not to be forgotten and not to be repeated.

THE BIG THREE

I WILL WRITE of three books in a category of their own, each of which became a household name. One sold 300,000 copies, another sold 600,000 copies, and the third sold 1,500,000 copies. Such figures are rare in publishing and especially in the field of picture books. We published all three as children's books and were sometimes accused of attempting to 'pass off' adult books for children. Certainly I am exceptionally proud of them and I believe each made a unique contribution to our culture. They gave pleasure to an enormous number of what I will call 'children of all ages'.

The Butterfly Ball and the Grasshopper's Feast

I begin with Alan Aldridge. He was appointed Art Director of Penguin Books when he was still in his mid-twenties. Alan was a magnificent draughtsman and, as an artist, he worked with a richness of colour the like of which I had never seen. It was these talents that led Penguin to believe he could give new life to their covers with a fresh and modern look. Alan had a striking appearance with a lean, handsome face and very long blond hair. He was one of the most imaginative artists I have ever worked with. It was doubtless this imagination that attracted the Beatles to his work. At the other extreme he

worked for Lord Snowdon, who invited him to lay out his photographic book. I recall Alan telling me a delightful story. While working in Snowdon's study, he heard the phone ring. He picked it up and the person on the end of the line asked to speak to Margaret. Alan said she had gone out. The message was: 'Please ask her to ring her sister.' It was the Queen.

Alan came to my office to discuss a book project he was tremendously excited by. He wanted to illustrate a Victorian children's book called *The Butterfly Ball and the Grasshopper's Feast*. The book was in verse and by a man called Roscoe but we both agreed that it was too old-fashioned and we would need a new text. Alan brought me the artwork for half a dozen plates. They were dazzlingly beautiful. He said that each plate had taken him a month to complete. Rather than asking for a large advance Alan wanted us to guarantee a first printing of 50,000 copies. I had complete confidence in his artwork but because we would have to commission a text, the project was a gamble. However, I was so excited by the pictures he had shown me that I agreed.

At that point we discussed a possible author and I told Alan that my first choice would be John Betjeman, a suggestion which filled him with joy. But I warned Alan that, from my limited knowledge of Betjeman, I felt he would be unlikely to take on the job. Our slim chance of success notwithstanding, I went off to see the old boy, taking with me Alan's pictures and the original text, with which, as I discovered, Betjeman was already familiar. Clearly our project appealed to him but he had a lot on and so he said, 'No.' Then he gazed again at the pictures and said, 'Maybe.' And then he gazed a while longer before finally saying, 'No.' He was really sorry. He looked as though he might well regret his decision, but did not change his mind again.

I had a different idea and that was to approach the poet William Plomer, a South African, who had moved to London many years previously. He was a reader at Jonathan Cape and I knew him extremely well, and I thought our project might appeal to him. He was not well off, so the income, if the book became the success I anticipated, would be welcome. William did not simply consent, he was thrilled to do so, and, to add to our delight, he began work almost immediately.

Meanwhile it took Alan the best part of a year to complete the illustrations. He would come to my office from time to time and on each occasion I grew even more convinced that publication would be a very big event. We decided to print the book with Pizzi, in Italy. They were particularly expensive but used special inks which would enable us to reproduce Alan's extravagant colours in facsimile. The result was a picture book of exceptional beauty. I took a copy home for my children, who were dazzled by the pictures and spent hours gazing at the details within them. Alan had incorporated several puzzles into his illustrations and these added to the pleasure to be found within.

The Butterfly Ball was subsequently featured in the *Sunday Times* colour supplement and written about at great length. Several critics described the book as a cornerstone of a new graphic revolution and even today, many years later, this remains true. *The Butterfly Ball and the Grasshopper's Feast* sold 300,000 copies.

The Human Body

The designer–artist David Pelham came into my life when we were both judging the D & AD Design Awards some twenty years ago. In casual conversation I asked David what he was planning to work on next. He picked up a paper napkin and, in his laidback way, scribbled a sketch which he pushed towards me. Then he went on to tell me a little more about his project. It was to be a pop-up with six spreads which would show, in three dimensions and with moving parts, the main functions of the human body. There would also be a text by Jonathan Miller. Harry Wilock would execute the artwork, but it was David who would draw everything first in the greatest possible detail. He would also make a paper model of the entire book (this is known as paper engineering) and the process would literally take thousands of hours. In an attempt to describe the complexity of the whole I must add that David's dummy would contain more than eighty 'glue points'. These are joins that have to be stuck together by hand, first by David for the dummy, and then by others at the factory for every single manufactured copy.

There are only two factories in the world which specialize in pop-ups. One is in Singapore and the other, called Carvehal, is in Colombia. David chose the latter, because he had worked with them in the past. It took him a year to complete his dummy and at that point I rang Colombia (which takes some doing) and told Carvehal that our dummy was ready to go. How much time would they need to produce an estimate? They reckoned our DHL package would take a week to reach

them and they would need a further two weeks to make their calculation. I waited four weeks and sent a fax asking when we might expect to hear. They faxed back saying they would need another week, it was a little more complicated than they had expected. Two weeks later we still had no estimate and I sent another fax. They replied that we would hear 'any day now'. Yet another two weeks passed (it was now eight weeks) and I faxed in an altogether different tone wanting to know what was going on. No answer. I had a hunch what might have happened. A man called Wally Hunt, the head of a Los Angeles company, InterVisual, the largest pop-up packagers in the world, might have got wind of our publication and leant on Carvehal to persuade them to refuse to produce the book unless we agreed to InterVisual's involvement. Since Wally Hunt's company was responsible for some 70 per cent of Carvehal's turnover it would be unwise to ignore his dictates. We had lost so much time by now that, deeply reluctantly, we decided 'to play ball'.

I fast-forward to publication. The *Human Body* was a triumph. Reviewers who had never before written about a pop-up devoted themselves to it at length. They praised both the contents and the artistic feat of imagination. It was infinitely the best non-fiction pop-up ever published. We sold more than 400,000 copies in the UK and more than a million overseas and it was translated into some twenty languages which, for a pop-up, was unheard of. And then came the ultimate accolade. I received a letter from the President of Colombia thanking me for the contribution we had made to the country's economy. I was invited to spend a week in Colombia. I still regret not having gone.

Masquerade

The third of the three books led to by far the strangest story as far as my life with picture books is concerned. The tale begins in the Portal Gallery, a place I frequented, which specialized in primitive art. One day I went in and saw a picture hanging on the back wall which was totally unlike any of the other paintings in the gallery or indeed any other painting I had ever seen. I asked for the name of the artist and learned it was Kit Williams, a name quite unfamiliar to me. His work was meticulous, rich in design and symbolism. He must have spent hundreds of hours working on the painting.

I was deeply intrigued and asked the gallery owner, Eric Lister, whether it would be possible to meet the artist, but he informed me that Kit Williams lived in Gloucestershire and very rarely came to London. No more than once a year. I said that was a pity because I thought his work might lend itself to an unusual book. On hearing this, Lister offered to drive me to see Kit Williams. It seemed a long way to go on a hunch but my hunch was so strong that I thought it would be worth making the journey, despite the fact that there was nothing at

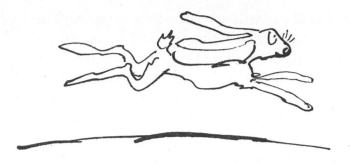

all about the painting to indicate that the artist could (or would want to) produce a children's book.

Some weeks later Lister and I set off to Gloucestershire and found Kit, who was most welcoming, waiting for us. He showed us several recent paintings, all impressive in a way similar to the one I had seen at the gallery. I told him that I was sure he could produce the most wonderful children's book, something that would be a beautiful object and would sell astonishingly well. He was rather irritated at the notion and said, 'You don't understand. If I were to produce a book the plates would have to have the same characters. That would bore me. With my paintings I am totally free to do anything I like. Each painting is a fresh experience.'

I found myself apologizing and dropped the subject until I left. Then I could not resist saying, 'It's a pity about the book. You could have produced a book like no other. A book that would have caught the imagination of the world. But never mind.' We drove back to London and I thought that was that.

Three months later Kit rang. He was in a high state of excitement, speaking quickly, mentioning a hare and a treasure and outlining a most complicated story. Eventually I managed to say, 'Last time I came to see you. This time you should come to see me.' And so he did, two weeks later. He explained the book he had in mind and then he said, 'I need £3,000 for the gold.' I was totally convinced. We gave him a contract and paid him the £3,000. The book was to be called *Masquerade*.

We waited exactly five years. I wrote a couple of letters just to cheer Kit on but we did not see each other. And then one day the phone rang and it was Kit, almost speechless with excitement: 'I've finished. When can I come?'

Two or three days later he arrived carrying what looked like a trunk. It was wrapped in a multi-coloured blanket and sewn up with heavy thread. 'This little lot is insured for £100,000,' Kit announced before he began to cut the thread and take out the pictures.

Each one was painted on wood, and all were exactly the same size. As the wonder of what I had begun to witness dawned on me, I invited a number of colleagues to come to my office. It was an experience I wanted to share. The paintings were incomparable in quality and each was framed with elaborate letters Kit had painted. If correctly interpreted, the words would lead to the precise location of the treasure, a golden hare, whilst those who failed to locate the treasure would find themselves in possession of a book which was in itself a treasure.

Masquerade generated a fervour of excitement such as I had never experienced. It began to sell instantaneously and we finally sold some 600,000 copies of the British edition alone. From the day of publication the entire phenomenon was written about without cease, as there was something about this book that caught the imagination of anyone who came into contact with it. Treasure hunters were to be found digging all over the country. I recall one woman ringing me to complain that her garden had been dug up because it was depicted in one of Kit's pictures. I also received many phone calls from people who assumed that I, as the publisher, could help them in their quest, whilst others called me because they had deciphered my name, which appeared in the tiniest letters (almost invisible to the human eye) on the side of a removal van in one of the paintings.

Meanwhile, an enterprising small American airline started *'Masquerade'* flights to the UK. And so it went on. We were offered numerous merchandizing deals from manufacturers of board games and jigsaw producers, not to mention the usual postcards, mugs, pottery, etc. Kit turned them all down and came to loathe the commercial aspects of what he had created. He had become a 'personality' and was in constant demand for television programmes, interviews and lectures, but his only wish, he declared, was to be left alone and return simply to being a painter. The story intrigued Bamber Gascoigne to such a degree that he wrote a book called *Quest for the Golden Hare*. Finally, three years after publication, someone deciphered the clues and found the treasure. That made the TV news.

We were credited with having devised the most imaginative and effective book promotion of all time. This was not so. The imagination was entirely that of the artist. He did not invent *Masquerade* in order to create a bestseller, but he did so, as he explained to me, in order to oblige the reader to look properly and in detail at his pictures.

KINGSLEY AMIS

ON THE FEW occasions I had met Kingsley Amis, I found him rather forbidding. He was invariably drunk and I am sure he would have no recollection of meeting me. To the world he was extremely famous as the author of *Lucky Jim*, one of the most celebrated novels of our time and also one of the funniest. I suspect, though, that Kingsley did not see himself as the least bit famous.

At the time of our first encounter Kingsley was married to Hilly and they had three young children: Philip, Martin and Sarah. Then, at the Cheltenham Festival, he met and fell in love with Elizabeth Jane Howard. I was not present but I remember this event almost to the day. At the time I was close to Jane and she rang me from Cheltenham, excited at having met Kingsley. They began to live together almost immediately, first in Maida Vale and later in a large country house with an enormous garden in Barnet. This was a compromise since Jane really wanted to be in the country and Kingsley wanted to be in London.

Jane was an 'old Cape author' (i.e. she had been published by Cape before my time). And she was by far the youngest and easiest to get on with in this category. Others included Elizabeth Bowen, C. Day-Lewis and the incomparable Ian Fleming.

Jane frequently invited me to join her and Kingsley for dinner. To my surprise I grew fond of the old boy and he seemed to like me too, although I represented the antithesis of what he most enjoyed. I was neither erudite nor especially witty, and – possibly my greatest defect from his point of view – I did not drink. I mean I did not drink seriously. Drink was something nearly all Kingsley's friends had in common, yet Kingsley was surprisingly disciplined about his booze. Special occasions apart, he would invariably hold off until 5.30 p.m. I often saw him glance at his watch from 5 p.m. onwards but he never weakened. The most important discipline for Kingsley was his writing schedule. All morning, all afternoon, daily until the appointed 5.30 p.m. And occasionally at weekends also. He worked with complete concentration, so much so that if the phone rang he could pick it up mid-sentence and when the conversation ended, he would put the phone down, continuing his sentence as though there had been no interruption.

To my delight Kingsley decided he wanted to be published by Cape and asked his agent (who by this time was the same as Jane's) to break the news to Gollancz, with whom he had always been. I had not even made an overture. Kingsley was far too alien a figure for me to approach in that way. But as we got to know each other even this changed and I found him to be tender and affectionate, sentimental and even tactile. He liked to hug and kiss men as much, perhaps even more, than

women. I should add that he did not have the slightest homosexual tendencies.

One day Kingsley invited me to join him and Jane on a
Mediterranean cruise aboard a small yacht they had chartered.
He seemed shy and almost embarrassed about it. I, of course,
was thrilled to accept. His generosity was such that he even
bought my return air ticket to Athens.

Now to a down side of Kingsley. Meticulous as he was
about his own writing, his attitude to literature was often
philistine, to put it mildly. Tolstoy, Chekhov and Dostoyevsky
all wrote 'piss'. (Although under protest Kingsley might admit
that this would perhaps not be applicable if you read them in
the original Russian.) Almost every 'foreign' book, whether
contemporary or not, was dismissed as 'crap'. This applied to
the whole of European literature, be it German (Thomas
Mann), French (Albert Camus) or Italian (Italo Calvino). Most
of the leading American writers, Saul Bellow to name but one,
were similarly condemned.

Given all this, I am not surprised that Kingsley thought so
little of his son Martin's work. What did surprise me was that
at a party at the Polish Club to celebrate the publication of one
of Martin's novels, Kingsley told Martin he found the book
unreadable, and he took the opportunity to add that he had
not got beyond the first few pages of *any* of Martin's novels.
This statement is so appalling that I would find it unbelievable
but for the fact that I was standing next to Martin. This
occurred at the time Kingsley had just split up with Jane and
moved in with his first wife Hilly and her husband. A strange
arrangement, this nevertheless seemed to work for all parties.
She looked after Kingsley and he paid the bills. Meanwhile
Martin made a point of inviting his father to dinner once a
week, a saintly act.

I have rarely met a man of so many contradictions as
Kingsley. He could be funny and joyous, yet he was basically

(and secretly) an unhappy man. His mood swings might explain his friendship with Philip Larkin. Then again it comes as a surprise that he loved music deeply. Not just jazz but classical music. Of course his other great passion was alcohol. He might indulge himself at the local pub (a frequent pursuit) or in what he called a 'decent' restaurant. The Mirabelle qualified and that is where I remember taking him on publication day of *Girl, 20*. Before the meal Kingsley consumed three double whiskies. These were followed by a bottle of Beaune, a bottle of Vosne Romanée and a bottle of Volnay. I helped a bit with the wines and he rounded off his meal with a Grand Marnier and a Courvoisier. Finally, believe it or not, he had a double glass of vintage port. I rang for a taxi. Kingsley did not just need help to the car. He needed to be carried into it. (Even when sober, Kingsley was incapable of hailing a taxi for himself. Strange as it may seem, he found the very act terrifying.)

As the taxi moved off to a seemingly ever-patient Jane I wondered what Kingsley would be thinking. Even in the state he was in, he might manage to muse about some development in his novel. But I thought that this time he had perhaps gone over the top, even by his standards, and in that event he would simply have fallen asleep.

SHORT PIECES ON
SOME NOVELISTS

EDNA O'BRIEN

Edna O'Brien was a wonderful fresh voice in our literature, well read, funny, and pretty too. She came from Ireland and this added a special lyrical quality to her work. I met her at the time of the publication of her first novel, *The Country Girls*. She was unhappy with her publisher and wanted to come to us with her second book, *The Lonely Girl*. We went on to publish her for many years. I think she liked being with us and I know everyone at Cape enjoyed publishing her. Then she wrote a novel set in an unnamed Eastern European country and its characters were tiny people, just a very few inches high. Edna delivered the book and, almost immediately, she went abroad. She left me a phone number and of course I rang her, suggesting we meet as soon as possible after her return to talk about the novel. I did not say how much I loved it. How could I? But I was as gentle as I knew how. The novel seemed to me unpublishable but of course I didn't say anything like that. However, Edna told various friends I had been incredibly cruel. She left us and went to Weidenfeld, where she published not this book (which has never been published) but another. From time to time I run into her but even now, so many years later, she will not look me in the eye.

FREDERIC RAPHAEL

Frederic Raphael is one of my oldest friends. In the early days, in the fifties, when we were both poor, I used to babysit for him from time to time. On one occasion, just before he and his wife Bee were going out to dinner, he came into the sitting room where I was reading a book. In his hand he held a small bunch of keys and he proceeded to lock first the writing desk and then a large bureau. I asked what he was doing, to which he replied, 'I'm locking up.' I told him there was no need to do that as I would not dream of going through his things. His response was: 'Why, aren't you interested?'

Freddy has a brilliant mind. He is a successful screenwriter as well as novelist. I suspect his film career has prevented him from becoming the 'serious novelist' he would like to be. With Freddy's brilliance comes an arrogance which he does not intend. Some years ago I especially admired a new book of his and wrote him a fan letter. His wife told me that for a period he kept my letter by his bedside in order to re-read it from time to time. I was most surprised, but also pleased and a little flattered.

PATRICK WHITE

Patrick White was clearly *the* great Australian novelist of our time. His books were on the grand scale and he was even compared to Tolstoy. His literary agent, Juliet O'Hea from Curtis Brown, felt he was not sufficiently appreciated by his then publisher and, knowing of my admiration for his work, she proposed that he move to Cape. My favourite of all White's novels is *Voss*, which reads like an adventure story of the very highest order.

Patrick was a tall and impressive figure. He had a craggy and unusually strong face. He had lived for many years with Manoly, a Greek, who had been his batman in the army. Unlike Patrick, a lover of art and music, Manoly was not sophisticated. They were clearly happy together.

Whilst Patrick secretly enjoyed his tremendous status in Australia, he constantly complained that he was 'bothered'. He wished that 'they' would leave him alone. And yet, when invited to dinner by the Prime Minister, he would always accept. This was just one of many such engagements.

It was important to Patrick that I should put in an appearance in Australia and so I visited him twice in Sydney, travelling there solely to see him. On each occasion, my trips were timed to coincide with his having just finished a new book. He liked me to read it on the spot, with which of course I complied. I would hole up in my hotel room for two days and at the end of that period, when I had finished reading the book, I would accept a dinner invitation to Patrick's house. Strangely, he was never especially interested in talking about the book. He just wanted to be sure that I had read it.

At Cape we were under orders to decline all prizes on Patrick's behalf. He believed these should be given to younger writers who needed the money, whereas he did not. Then, in 1973 he won the Nobel Prize, over which we had no control. He hesitated as to whether he would accept the prize (eventually deciding he would) or not. He did not hesitate about whether he would go to Stockholm for the ceremony. He made a point of declining, asking his friend, the Australian painter Sidney Nolan, to go on his behalf.

NADINE GORDIMER

By the time Nadine Gordimer joined Cape she was very highly rated and it was flattering that she should choose us as her new publisher. But she was not undemanding. Whenever she came to London we took her and her husband out to dinner, or Regina would cook for them at home. Naturally if we invited other guests we would be at pains to choose someone special. On one occasion we invited Roald and Liccy Dahl. Nadine and Roald were both considerable personalities and neither of them could be called an 'easy person'. They took an instant dislike to each other. The problem was in part 'political' but also simply a clash of personalities. It was not long into the evening before we realized that we had perpetrated some kind of act of folly. As the meal progressed this became more and more apparent, until with the arrival of dessert, Roald, obviously planning a quick getaway, asked us to order him a taxi. This we duly did and we were told that the car would be with us in ten minutes. After twenty-five minutes Roald considered the delay excessive and we rang another company, whose car arrived fifteen minutes later. Waiting for Roald's cab did not improve the evening.

On the whole Nadine seemed pleased with Cape's performance. The one thing that drove her crazy was to find misprints in a novel, and I don't blame her. Sometimes there were several, which invariably crept in after the proof had been corrected, in other words they were the printer's errors and out of our control. Now, when Nadine gave me the manuscript of *The Conservationist*, she said: 'I do not want to see a single misprint in this book and there is one page where you must be particularly careful.' I don't recall the exact page, but I do remember that the one to which we alerted the printer was the very page that went wrong.

Nadine left us, although it was not solely due to this, nor indeed to the dinner with the Dahls. Shortly thereafter, in 1991, she won the Nobel Prize. Over the years we had been her principal publisher but on this occasion I had no desire to go to Stockholm.

ANITA BROOKNER

Anita Brookner is a very fine writer. Although she has won the Booker Prize (which led to enormous sales of *Hotel du Lac*) she does not have the readership she deserves. As a person she is enigmatic. We would have a traditional lunch to celebrate the publication of each new book, but that was about it. We talked of literature and of France but there was no question of anything personal. Once she mentioned that she was reading Proust for the fourth time. I asked cautiously, 'In French?'

'Of course,' she said.

Now, I have a love for Proust, and his work gives me the greatest pleasure, and yet I must confess that having made several starts in English I have still not reached the final volume. Anita's *four* times in French seems to me an astonishing achievement.

Despite our relatively formal relationship, I felt she was fond of me and I certainly have a considerable affection for her. Nevertheless, when the moment came for Liz Calder, the colleague with whom I 'shared' Anita, to leave, I assumed Anita would choose to follow her. Given her private nature, I did not like to ask and I suspect that Liz didn't either. One day someone in our publicity department mentioned that Anita was up in the boardroom signing her latest book and she wondered whether I wanted to say hello. I went up and began opening books for Anita to sign. I did so for about a quarter of an hour, during which she signed in silence. And then, after closing the last book, she turned to me and said, 'Tom, I want you to know that I shall be staying with you.'

IAN FLEMING

At the time I joined Cape there was one 'star' on our list. It was Ian Fleming, author of the James Bond books. The books sold well (15,000–20,000 copies) but, to my surprise, not momentously well. Equally surprising to me was the fact that Fleming was revered by a number of our classiest reviewers. Cyril Connolly, of the *Sunday Times*, for example, was a fan. Personally I enjoyed reading the Bond books and thought Fleming spun a good yarn. But I must confess I didn't really rate them as literature.

I cannot say that I got to know Ian Fleming at all well though I met him numerous times in the office and sometimes also at lunch. I was even on occasion invited to dinner at Fleming's house by Annie, his wife, who was one of the best-known hostesses of the time. Fleming was a tall, august figure, meticulously dressed and invariably to be seen holding a long cigarette holder. I have always thought he might have been a spy with that plastic face of his. He looked more like a banker than a writer. Fleming took his books very seriously and researched them meticulously. It meant more to him that they should be respected than that they should sell in large numbers. So, when it came to my suggesting to Tony Colwell that we should have a big campaign for the first Bond book to be published in my time, Fleming was relatively indifferent (this in spite of the fact that we increased his sales by 50 per cent). He was strangely obsessed with a need to deliver his new book exactly one year from the delivery date of his previous one. It was not until the first Bond film (*Dr No*, in 1962) that the books became prodigiously successful. The films were made by two buccaneers, Harry Saltzman and Cubby Broccoli. Numerous film producers before them had pronounced Bond books too fanciful and unfilmable, but Saltzman and Broccoli decided to make the films every bit as fanciful as the books. The result was a triumph from the first film to the last. Although we, as publishers, were relatively insignificant in the process, we collaborated to some extent with the producers on promotion. It was my role to spend very many hours in Harry Saltzman's office 'having a meeting' with him, which consisted of my listening to interminable conversations he conducted with various studios in Hollywood. Harry seemed oblivious of the fact that these conversations were completely irrelevant to me. It was simply that he liked to have an audience.

YURI MUCHA

Yuri Mucha was the son of the great Art Nouveau designer. He was a novelist and he lived in both London and Prague. He had told me that if I ever visited Prague I must not fail to look him up. The other author I knew there (and only very slightly) was Václav Havel, the President. I was his original publisher in England when he was a famous playwright, long before taking high office.

On the whole I do not indulge in literary pilgrimages. But for me Kafka was an exception and it was he that took me to Prague. I walked the beautiful city on a sentimental journey, passing cafés full of animated people and especially of pretty young girls. I found the girls difficult to approach. When I visited Mucha I mentioned this to him. He said he thought he could be of assistance. He wrote down an address and suggested I appear there the following evening at 8 p.m. I did so and found a small drinks party in progress. Later on – it must have been about 9 p.m. – Yuri stood in the middle of the room and said, 'Let's go.' He began to take off his clothes and so did everyone else. That is how it began. People lay down on the sofas, on the armchairs, on the carpet. They fondled one another and sometimes they fondled two people at once. And then they began to make love and having made love to one person they turned their attention to another. There were many more girls than men and they were as pretty and as young as those I had seen in the cafés. It was surprising to find all this in the city of Kafka.

RUSSELL HOBAN

Russell Hoban, whom I mentioned earlier, writes superb novels for adults and wonderful stories for children. His children's stories include *Captain Nojark*, and the adult books include *Riddley Walker*. This book was hailed as a masterpiece in several newspapers including the *Observer*. Russell would agree with this opinion.

From time to time Russsell wrote a short text for a picture book and I took a delight in 'marrying' him with the right illustrator, matching him at one time with Quentin Blake and at another with Nicola Bayley. I think it might be said that I served him well, especially given the fact that he refused to budge from a 50/50 split. He will hold out for half the advance and half the royalties, totally disregarding the fact that whilst a writer may spend a few days producing four or five pages of text, the illustrator might take six months or more for the pictures. It was a pleasure to publish Russell and there was always an element of surprise as to what he would come up with next. One could be certain it would be extremely well written and in his uniquely knotty style.

Russell speaks in a manner similar to the one in which he writes, which makes it a joy to be in his company. He seemed to enjoy my company also. Certainly he told me that he thought I was a wonderful publisher and I do not believe this was entirely because I admired his work.

Sometimes we would lunch alone while at other times we would have dinner at his home or mine, together with our wives, Gundl and Regina. So there was also a social side to our relationship. Russell liked to talk of film and television, but not about books, for he claimed to enjoy only one writer and that was Stephen King. Others, he said, did not interest

With Len Deighton and friend at Carney

We play the mud game at Kurt Vonnegut's house in Cape Cod

Kurt Vonnegut with the very young Hannah

At Belmont House, Lyme Regis, together with John Fowles

At the annual
Cape authors' party,
from left to right,
me, Elizabeth
Jane Howard,
Kingsley Amis
and John Lennon

With Desmond
Morris at his
villa in Malta

Edna O'Brien and John Fowles at Carney

At Roald Dahl's seventieth-birthday party, with Liccie, center, and Roald

Quentin Blake at my apartment in SW London

Picador Anniversary party (1982). From left to right:
Tim Binding, Michael Herr, Salman Rushdie, Bruce Chatwin,
Clive James, Adam Mars Jones, Mike Petty, Russell Hoban, Hugo Williams,
Sonny Mehta, Oliver Sacks; sitting, me and Emma Tennant

Kit Williams,
centre, with
(left to right)
the man who
found the treasure,
Kit's wife, me and
Rupert Lancaster,
our publicity
director

With Elizabeth
Jane Howard and
Kingsley Amis on
a Mediterranean
yacht trip

Jeffrey was convinced that his earnings made an incalculable contribution to the success of Jonathan Cape

I begged to differ

Philippe de Rothschild with Joan Littlewood at Mouton

Ian McEwan at Les Aspres on the occasion of my sixtieth-birthday party

A dinner given in London by Julian Barnes for my birthday.
From left: Martin Amis, me, Regina and Ian McEwan

Above and left:
Carney

Allen Ginsberg
on the hill
above Carney

Asking Mohammed Ali
for his autograph

With Wilfred Thesiger
at the Hay Festival

Peter Mayle comes over to see the second-century grave which we have found some 200 yards from our house

Hannah, Ben and Alice at a party given by Gail Rebuck to celebrate my forty years in publishing

Les Aspres

him, though I was unsure how he could know this since he appeared never to have tried any of them.

And then Russell sent us a new novel called *Angelica's Grotto*. I liked it, as I like almost everything he writes, but I did not love it. Certainly I would have taken the book on had I still been in charge. I gave the manuscript to our Literary Director, Dan Franklin, who felt we should turn it down. Perhaps if I had been more passionately in favour I might have persuaded Dan.

Some months later I ran into Russell at one of the Chris Beetles Gallery launch parties. He saw me and nodded in my direction but did not approach. I nodded back. Some time later I could see Russell making his way towards me. I concentrated the harder upon the people to whom I was talking, but when the group broke up, I could no longer escape Russell. There he stood at my elbow. He waited and then he struck: 'You know, I want to thank you for turning down *Angelica's Grotto*. You did me an enormous favour. It is so good to be with Bloomsbury. They really love my work.'

JEFFREY ARCHER

THE LITERARY AGENT Deborah Owen (wife of the politician David Owen) sent me a manuscript, *Not a Penny More, Not a Penny Less* by an unknown author, Jeffrey Archer. She did not actually say it was a first submission but, in the manner of certain agents content to mislead, this was the implication. The aspect of Archer's book which especially intrigued me was that he had himself been involved in a con and had lost a great deal of money, both his own and others'. And now he had written a thriller about a man similar to himself, and furthermore was doing so in order to earn a large sum so that the money lost could be repaid. Certainly that is what he claimed. I found the conceit intriguing, and although the style was indifferent, decided to offer a contract. I must admit I was motivated, in part, by the feeling that Jeffrey was so obviously ambitious that he would be likely to succeed in almost anything to which he put his mind. This has, of course, turned out to be the case in his writing if not in his political career.

Not a Penny More, Not a Penny Less was not an enormous moneymaker but it marked the beginning of what was to become a prodigiously successful career. If Archer has a special place in my publishing life it lies in the fact that he is the only immensely commercial writer I have 'discovered'. I possess a copy of *Not a Penny More, Not a Penny Less* inscribed by Archer with the words: 'as much your achievement as mine'.

As we shall see, it was not to be a long-lasting relationship. I have put 'discovered' in inverted commas because, although the notion is commonly held by publishers, it is almost always a misnomer. In my opinion publishers do not discover writers, they come across them. *Not a Penny More* was followed by the thriller *Shall We Tell the President?*, based upon the assassination of Bobby Kennedy. We paid twice as much for the second book as for the first, £5,000, and it was even more successful although not at all in the league of what was to follow.

During the course of publishing *Shall We Tell the President?* I began to observe Jeffrey's ambition. For example, he let it be known that he was not too proud to appear on almost any television programme if and when a last-minute vacancy occurred. Producers could count on him and they did. The result of course was that Jeffrey appeared on television more frequently than almost anyone else, which in turn helped promote his book.

On one occasion I recall finding myself on the railway station at Reading, where I had been visiting my old school, Leighton Park. At the station there was a bookstall displaying books by only one author: Jeffrey Archer. The books were all face out and I could not resist asking the manager how this had come about. He told me that Jeffrey had taken the trouble to invite him to lunch and the display was nothing but returning a favour.

My favourite Jeffrey Archer story is one I *can* be sure of because it occurred just between the two of us. Jeffrey confided in me that he greatly admired *The French Lieutenant's Woman* by John Fowles, so much so that he had read it four times. He went on to ask whether I thought that if he read the book a further four times he might, just might, have a chance of winning the Nobel Prize. Not the Booker Prize. The Nobel Prize. Now, how do you answer a question like that?

This brings us to the moment of truth in my relationship with Jeffrey Archer. Deborah Owen rang to say Jeffrey had finished his new (third) novel. It was called *Kane and Abel* and she was about to send it to me. However, she wanted to alert me to the fact that Jeffrey required a lot of money for this book. The novel duly arrived and I read just a few pages in the office (I hardly ever have time to read anything there). Even with so little to go on I could easily sense the makings of a big bestseller. So I determined that four key people at Cape should read the book and we would meet to discuss it as soon as possible.

Each one of us found the book immensely readable. This included me and I was the hardest to please. In the light of Deborah Owen's statement I calculated that she would be looking for anything between £25,000 and £50,000. Whilst there was no doubt that *Kane and Abel* would become an enormous commercial success, there was equally no doubt that it was not 'a Cape book'. We have always had lower literary standards for thrillers, but this was a family saga. None the less I argued we should try to buy the rights. Our reputation was such that we were hardly ever offered strictly commercial books, and here we had one on our doorstep so to speak. I proposed that we should show our confidence by offering £50,000 rather than a smaller sum, as this would oblige us to get behind the book in a big way. Everyone agreed: £50,000 it was to be. I couldn't wait to get on the phone to Debbie. 'We've decided to offer fifty thousand,' I blurted out. This was greeted with: 'Oh. Wait a minute.' Taken aback, I replied, 'You cannot tell me that you were looking for more?' 'No, no, it isn't that. I must talk to Jeffrey.' It occurred to me at this moment that Deborah might have been hoping for so inadequate an offer that it would be easy for Jeffrey to break his option with us and go elsewhere. I had to wait three days for her response and when it came she said, 'Jeffrey wants to know whether you really admire the book.'

'That is going too far,' I replied. 'Fifty thousand, yes, but you can't expect me to perjure myself. For me to truly love the book the writing would have to be of a totally different order. And furthermore I'm willing to bet, Debbie, that you, in your heart of hearts, don't love the book any more than I do.' And so terminated the relationship which had been as brief as it had been unique for me.

WILDLIFE

I HAVE ALWAYS been fascinated by wildlife and so naturally, as a publisher, I took a special interest in animal books. Unfortunately a rival publisher, William Collins, had something of a monopoly in the field, which came about as a result of his publishing one of the most successful wildlife books of our time: *Elsa: The True Story of a Lioness.* So I had to make do with smaller fry.

My first animal book was by Arjan Singh. He is a famous conservationist, particularly in India. He lived alone in a small wooden house in the jungle in northern Uttar Pradesh, on the border of Nepal. From Delhi it was an exhausting train journey of some twenty hours, and quite an adventure. The leopard in this area had been preyed upon by both hunters and poachers and was now endangered. Singh determined to find out whether it would be possible to raise a leopard cub in his home and then return it to the jungle. For the animal to survive he would have to teach it the way of the jungle, a difficult task, and yet this is what he achieved. He did so with a leopard called Prince, who became the hero of the book called *Prince of Cats* which we published.

On one occasion I stayed with Arjan Singh for five days, and during this time I spent many hours walking through the jungle with him. He never carried a gun and was so confident that it did not occur to me to be afraid. In the evenings, when we were not out walking, he would tell me stories. One of them concerned a female leopard, Harriet, whom he had taken into his home. Later she left for the jungle where she gave birth to cubs. At the time of the monsoon floods, she carried the cubs back to his house one by one and installed them in his bedroom.

The Prince of Cats was followed by a biography of John Aspinall. He owned two zoos and devoted his life to animals, proudly stating that he much preferred them to humans. Whilst he did not have independent means he owned several gambling clubs and it was with the earnings from these that he financed his animal exploits. While we were working on the book, Aspinall invited Regina and me to lunch at his zoo, Howletts. One of his zoo keepers had recently been killed by an elephant and Aspinall obviously felt remorse. The public outcry was such that it would have been impossible not to, but he did say that the odd accident was inevitable.

Before lunch he took us on a tour of the zoo. The cleanliness was most impressive and the zoo seemed a happy place. We passed a banana branch, some twelve feet high and thick with glistening fruit. The bananas were so tempting that I asked if I might have one. 'Certainly not,' Aspinall said, 'they have only just arrived from Harrods this morning and are for the gorillas.' Two baby gorillas were new to the zoo and we went to visit them. They lived in a small house with the young lady who looked after them. The gorillas were the size of a four-year-old child and wore nappies. Aspinall said it was safe to pick them up. I held one and Regina held the other and hers then caught hold of her necklace and twisted and twisted with enormous force until it broke.

Limited as it has been, my publishing in the animal field gave me a taste – I should say a passion – for seeing animals in the wild. It is easy to see lions and cheetahs and giraffes and buffaloes and crocodiles. But there are two animals, both rare, by which I have been particularly enthralled. The first is the mountain gorilla, of which there remain but 700 or so in the world.

Regina and I travelled to Bwindi in Uganda in search of the gorilla. It is not an easy journey. We flew to Entebbe and continued by Land Rover, an eighteen-hour journey on rough roads. Considering its extreme remoteness, the camp at Bwindi was surprisingly comfortable. Our tent looked straight out on to a tree-covered mountain where the gorillas lived. On the first day, we assembled at 7 a.m. Everything was highly organized. There are two trekking groups a day, each of six people, never more, and we were told that from the moment we came upon a gorilla family, assuming that we did so, we would be allowed just one hour in their presence. With us came a guide, three men with machine-guns and two assistants. The machine-guns are of course for protection against guerrillas. This precaution was put in place just after the massacre which had taken place two years previously.

Trekking gorillas is an endurance test. The incline of the mountains is 45 degrees. To come upon the animals, sur-rounded by jungle, is the most marvellous experience in the world. We had booked for two days (you have to book many months in advance) and we were fortunate enough to see a gorilla family on each day, first a family of nine, with one silverback male, and then one of fourteen, with two. The young hopped about like joyous children while the males moved slowly, gently, or simply lay on their backs. They were even larger than I had imagined, and it was wonderful to be able to get so close to them, within a distance of a mere ten feet. The experience made me feel elated, privileged.

This brings me to a tiger adventure, both an animal story and a travel tale. I had gone to India with a friend, Sarah Giles, who was as keen to see tigers as I was. Sarah is exceedingly well connected and we started our journey by staying in the palace of the Maharajah of Jaipur, at the invitation of his son, Jagat. During our visit he drove us to the family hunting lodge, which is situated in an idyllic landscape some forty miles outside Jaipur, where they used to hunt tigers. On our second day I asked Jagat if it would be possible to buy some marijuana. 'Of course,' he said, 'give the boy ten rupees [about ten pence] and he will get it this afternoon.' That afternoon, the boy duly arrived with the most enormous plastic bag full to the brim. I wondered what I could do with such a large amount of the stuff.

Then we left for the game park, Kahna, where we hoped to find tigers. This is best done on elephant-back, as the tigers are accustomed to the smell of elephants and therefore undisturbed by them. Sarah and I arranged to meet our *mahout* (the man who takes care of the elephant) at 5.30 a.m. the following day. The plan was to be under way before sunrise. On day one we found some tracks but no tigers. On the second day we saw a tiger, but only fleetingly, for he was on the move. On the third day we were fortunate and came upon a tiger with a kill. (We did not see him make the kill, which would have been even more exciting, but I am told this is very rare.) Our tiger stayed with his kill for an hour or so and we were able to watch him as he worked on it. And then, slowly and elegantly, he got up and disappeared into the high grass.

When we returned to the lodge we saw another elephant with two men sitting upon him. At the elephant's feet a group of children were gathered, gesticulating and waving pieces of paper. I asked Sarah what was going on. She had immediately recognized the men and explained that they were the cricketers David Gower and Graham Gooch. The children had obviously also recognized them (unlike me) and were clamouring for autographs. Sarah mentioned that she really fancied David Gower's cricket cap (she may also have fancied David Gower, who was extremely good-looking). We approached

our compatriots, still on their elephant, and learned that they were spending the night in our lodge, so we would see them later. That evening we had a drink together and I took the opportunity of offering David Gower a fine bottle of white Burgundy, hard to find in India, in exchange for his cap. He did not need any persuasion!

Back in London, I read about the disastrous test match that took place a few days after our evening with Gower and Gooch. The Indians had wiped out the English team.

LAUREN BACALL

I DO NOT MAKE a habit of publishing the memoirs of film stars. Indeed, this situation has only arisen twice in my life. On the first occasion the publication itself was a great success but the author, alas, tremendously disappointing. The person in question is none other than Lauren Bacall. We had acquired the publishing rights in her book, *Lauren Bacall By Myself*, via an auction, which was an unusual procedure for us (Cape tended to avoid auctions since one is frequently driven to pay more than a book is worth). But Lauren Bacall, or Betty as her friends call her, seemed irresistible, especially because the book had a particular quality derived from the fact that she had written it personally. I know this because Bob Gottlieb assured me that she wrote a great deal of the book in the Knopf offices. Beyond the fact that Bacall wrote the book herself, it had the special attraction of detailing her marriage to Humphrey Bogart. The two sections in the book that most delighted me were those covering her youth and the early days of their love affair. And, most moving of all, was Bacall's description of Bogart's cancer which finally killed him. Here she wrote with a love and tenderness difficult to reconcile with the woman we were to meet.

Naturally we had all been hopeful that Bacall would come over to promote her book. She agreed to this provided we paid for first-class travel and accommodation, a perfectly reasonable request. What I found much less reasonable was her insistence that we pay for her hairdresser to accompany her, not simply to the UK, but also to Australia where Bacall was due to spend a mere three to four days. I tried to talk her out of the latter condition but she was adamant, seeming to ignore the fact that a medium-sized publishing house lacks the resources of a large US film studio.

This brings me to her car. Naïve as we were, we *did* realize that the company Volvo would fall far short of Betty's expectations. And so, with pride and joy, we hired a Mercedes limousine. On the day after Bacall's arrival we sent the car to the Connaught to pick her up and bring her to our extremely elegant Bedford Square offices. I shall not forget the disdain with which she pointed through the window and announced that our Mercedes was not what she had in mind. It was a stretch limo she required and furthermore it was only in such a vehicle that she would return to the Connaught.

The car episode was mild in comparison with what was to follow. I have never before encountered such behaviour. Let me restrict myself to one especially painful example. A television company in Bristol and another in Glasgow were both keen to have Bacall appear on a particular day. The only way the two of them could be fitted into her schedule was by our chartering a small plane. By publishing standards this was most extravagant but I agreed to it. Marilyn Edwards, who was in charge of publicity, had been looking after Betty since her arrival in London, and she put the plan to her. To our amazement, Bacall announced that she could not possibly accept a four-seater plane unless there were two pilots. Marilyn asked me whether we could run to a second pilot. I refused. It seemed excessive. Knowing that Marilyn had her own concerns about flying, I suggested she try Bacall again, making the point that small planes are, by all accounts, safer than large ones. Bacall had no intention of modifying her view. When Marilyn said she was very willing to overcome her own fears of flying with small planes, Bacall countered with a memorable and to my mind horrendous statement: 'Well, it's all very well for you, dear, but what if something were to happen to me?' I cannot swear as to the exact words but there is no doubt about her meaning. Needless to say, we cancelled the TV programmes and the flight also.

Two days later, I came into the Publicity Department at about 6 p.m. and found everyone drinking champagne. 'Whose birthday?' I asked jauntily. It was no one's birthday. They were simply drinking to Bacall's departure.

I cannot resist a postscript. Just after writing the above, a little item caught my eye in the *Sunday Times*. After agreeing to attend a charity gala for the Woman's Project at an all-female New York theatre event, Bacall sent a last-minute request. She expected no payment for turning up, but she did want $2,000 for her hair and make-up. This item appeared twenty-five years after her visit to us.

*

THIS BRINGS ME to my second and only other 'star' experience. The subject, this time, was Elizabeth Taylor. Her agent, Robbie Lantz in New York, who had three years previously introduced me to Carson McCullers, now mentioned that his client Elizabeth Taylor was ready to write her autobiography. He asked whether I would be interested. How could one resist? In addition to Taylor, there were two husbands of particular interest. Mike Todd had caught my imagination while I was at school and I remember mourning his death when he crashed his plane. I also remember a particular statement of his that stuck in my mind: 'I owe five million dollars and I should smoke smaller cigars.' The other Taylor husband was so attractive to her that she married him twice. It was of course Richard Burton. Living in the Vale of Health, in Hampstead, at the beginning of my career in publishing, I used to see the Burtons regularly for they had rented a small house a few hundred yards away from ours, on East Heath Road, and made quite a sight holding each other on the edge of the Heath.

The date was set for me to meet Elizabeth Taylor on her next visit to London, and I was invited for a drink at her suite in the Savoy. There I found a petite figure almost totally obscured by flowers. Rarely have I met such an instantly warm and gracious celebrity. She told me she wanted to work with a ghost-writer friend of hers. I can't say I was convinced but I expressed enthusiasm. The terms of the contract were reasonable and so we went ahead. The writer was unwilling to show me any work in progress and, alas, when the book arrived I thought it so badly written that I felt obliged to ask to be released from the contract. It was not simply that I was disappointed but, having liked Elizabeth Taylor so much, I felt I had failed her. We were left only with a double-page spread in our catalogue, one page describing the book and another with a ravishing photograph.

SWIFTY AND
ARTUR RUBINSTEIN

THE NAME, or at least the nickname, was known to everyone in the film and literary world. His real name was Irwin Lazaar, but most people knew him as Swifty. The first picture I ever saw of him was in *Time* magazine. The photograph showed his dinner-party companion in the process of smashing a gold goblet on to Swifty's bald pate.

He dealt mainly with the movie world, representing film stars and also handling book properties. Here he developed a spectacular technique. He might ring up, say, Laurence Olivier (whom he was not representing) and announce that he had been offered half a million dollars for Olivier's autobiography. After putting down the phone from that particular conversation he would then call a publisher and claim he was representing Olivier, arguing that half a million dollars would purchase the rights in his autobiography.

I had been a publisher for many years before encountering this legend. When in London he always stayed at Claridges. It was from there that he rang me, announcing that in New York he 'had' (he did business with) just two publishers: Tom Guinsberg and Bob Gottlieb. This for him represented one chic and one scruffy publisher. In London he had George

Weidenfeld as the chic publisher and from what he had been told I might be a candidate for the scruffy one.

Once I was present upon Swifty's arrival at Claridges. He opened one of his cases and handed the concierge an enormous pair of double sheets to be used on his bed, his phobia for cleanliness extending even to this august hotel.

Swifty wasted no time suggesting that we might meet and came straight to the point. He had something to sell and if I lived up to my reputation I would buy it. The price was $100,000 and the article was the legendary pianist Artur Rubinstein's memoirs. Knowing of Swifty's reputation for selling film rights without even allowing the purchaser to read the book, I asked tentatively if I might see the manuscript. Permission granted. The book arrived on my desk within the hour. I read as much as I needed to that evening and felt the book was not worth anything like $100,000. I rang him early the following day to say so – I felt I might as well get some credit for acting fast. I was expecting Swifty to be irritated, but not at all. He simply wanted me to return the manuscript without delay.

It was some nine months before I heard from him again. His opening words were: 'Say, kid, I've been thinking. The Rubinstein memoirs are yours for just half of what I wanted' (obviously, 'I've been thinking' meant he had approached a number of other publishers). In my opinion, half was still far too much and so I countered with: 'If you said half of half I might be interested.' Quick as a flash the answer came back, 'Done.' I was startled. Now I was faced with two alternatives. I could either point out that I had not actually offered half of half or I could simply accept the deal. It might get me in with the great man. I thought briefly and accepted, although I did add one significant condition, which was that Artur Rubinstein should spend three days promoting the book at the time of publication. Swifty accepted on behalf of Rubinstein, provided only that the days should tie in with a London concert.

And so it was that I rang the maestro at the Savoy shortly after his arrival in London. He was extremely diffident, and I fully expected that he would have no idea who I was. He was clearly entirely caught up with thoughts of his concert. But then the book registered and, although he did not wish to undertake anything at all until after the concert, he said, 'I am at your disposal for three days from seven a.m. the day after the performance.'

In the light of his advanced age (he was ninety-three) we kept activities to a minimum: one television programme, a few press interviews and a book signing. The latter was at Hatchard's and heavily promoted. I duly collected our author from the Savoy but on arrival in Piccadilly, I was appalled by what I saw. The shop was packed out, with just enough room for a small desk in a corner. Outside there was an enormous queue which reached down towards Hyde Park Corner and broke all records, even for a Hatchard's signing. Inside, Artur sat straight back in his chair and, not content with simply signing his name, he invariably added the name of the person for whom the book was dedicated. This he did extremely slowly and it would have taken at least a week for him to sign for everyone. Looking both distinguished and frail, he turned to me – I was holding the books open for him – and with his big smile he said, 'You know, I have never done this before.' I felt terrible, almost as though I had tricked him into it. In my defence I must say a signing session is such a routine matter that it was reasonable to assume even Artur Rubinstein would have been subjected to it from time to time. He was not the least bit reproachful, but having done just over an hour he was clearly exhausted and we had to call a halt. I apologized to his fans and remember admiring the generosity with which they accepted the situation. I must add that Artur volunteered to

sign a further 100 copies if we sent them over to his hotel. The signing session apart, the publication of *My Many Years* was a triumph and the success of the book was such that we earned far more than the heavily debated advance! Rubinstein was pleased and so was Swifty.

In fact Swifty was so pleased that to my delight, and also my surprise, he invited my wife and me to spend a few days with him in his Los Angeles home. Most generously he lent us his car and chauffeur (or one of them). Of this stay I have three particular memories. First, there was a Hollywood dinner party in our honour. The guests included Cary Grant and I recall being surprised that he looked exactly like Cary Grant. I was also surprised that the dinner party, made up entirely of movie people, felt exactly like the average London dinner party. My second memory is of rows of lights on the telephones at our bedside which did not cease to flash all through the night. Our host must have been engaged in non-stop business around the world while others were sleeping. This brings me to the third memory, of which I am thoroughly ashamed. Swifty had a collection of paintings in which he took great pride. It was what I call a one-of-each collection. In other words, one Matisse, one Cézanne, one Dufy, one Picasso and so on. Each picture seemed to have been selected in order to impress or because it fitted into a particular colour scheme and certainly not because it had the capacity to move its owner. And so we come to my faux pas. Among Swifty's paintings there were two – a Modigliani and a Renoir – which looked to me as though they might not be right, and I had the temerity to suggest to Swifty that perhaps he should have them checked. Of course he was very angry and he was right to be so.

Swifty died in 1993 and I have often wondered what happened to his most gentle and beautiful wife Mary.

SOME AUTOBIOGRAPHICAL PIECES

PHILIPPE DE ROTHSCHILD

Philippe de Rothschild's autobiography was published in France under the title *Digne Ma Vigne*. Most of his family were in banking, and had been for a century, but Philippe chose the château in Bordeaux and the making of the great Mouton Rothschild wines. At the time he came into my life his wife Pauline had recently died, and he preserved her bedroom, on the first floor of the château, exactly the way she had left it. When I met him, however unlikely it may seem, he was living with Joan Littlewood. I say 'unlikely' because Joan, the famous director of the Theatre Royal, Stratford, in the East End of London, swore, drank and was on the far left. Of those with whom she had worked the playwright with whom she seemed the most comfortable was the iconoclastic Irishman Brendan Behan. Philippe, as one might expect, was elegant and aristocratic and I would no more have expected Joan to be attracted to him than vice versa.

It was in London that Joan told me about 'the old boy' and his book. The writing, she said, was 'lousy' but she was willing to translate the book and also to rewrite it. When she had a complete draft, she invited me down to the château and I spent four nights there. Philippe was, of course, proud of his vineyard but he was even more so of his *caves*. The *caves* I had known previously consisted of a room or perhaps even several rooms in which wine was stored. In Philippe's case they were made up of cellar after cellar and they must have run for miles. It would take an hour to walk the full length of them. He showed me round, and as we passed, say, the 1924, he would remark he was down to 800 bottles. Of the 1947 he still had perhaps 1,700 bottles, or in the case of the '61 it was 2,000.

In the mornings Joan and I would work on the book and in the afternoons we strolled around the property which bordered on to that of some of the other great wine growers. I was fascinated to learn from her about the competition between the great châteaux: Mouton, Lafite, Latour. At the time of the harvest each vineyard would send out spies to report back on precisely what the neighbours were up to. The art of when to pick the grapes was even greater than that of the precise composition of the soil. While strolling around the

vineyard Joan and I talked about a possible title for the English edition of the book and she suggested *Mi Lady Vine*.

Of course the high point of my stay was the evening meal, and not for the food. Philippe would spend a good deal of time early in the day with the sommelier and together they would arrive at a selection, dating from 1910 to 1960. Unlikely as it may seem, six bottles were chosen and every one of them would be consumed. Philippe drank no more than half a bottle. Joan and I drank the rest. What an experience! I have never before (or since) had the opportunity of consuming so much great wine, and totally regardless of cost. I must add that to my great surprise, no matter how much I drank, I did not have the least sign of a hangover.

YVES SAINT LAURENT

I learned that Yves Saint Laurent was ready to write his autobiography. My knowledge of the fashion world is exceedingly limited but this was a name even I knew. And the fact that Saint Laurent had become head of the House of Dior aged twenty-one had caught my imagination. He had taken to drugs early in his life but I was assured he had given them up, and I supposed that he could now concentrate on the autobiography to which he aspired. He certainly had a wonderful story to tell. To my surprise we were able to buy the rights for a reasonable sum and when the contract was signed I was invited by Pierre Berger (Saint Laurent's ex-lover and subsequent business partner) to lunch at the Athenaeum in Paris. He also invited the writer they had chosen to work with Saint Laurent. There we agreed that the first fifty pages would be sent to me within three months for my comments. At the end of lunch Berger took from his pocket a large wad of 500-franc notes, held the pile with his left hand while he peeled off notes with his right and doled them out to the numerous individuals who had attended us. I gathered that he lunched at the Athenaeum almost daily.

After a year and a half I had still not received a single page of the book. Meanwhile, Berger had bought a house at Saint-Rémy, not far from our French home. It became evident that the book would never happen and so we decided to cancel the contract. For once we got our money back but I would much prefer to have published the book. I would have also liked to meet Saint Laurent, which I never did.

NOËL COWARD

We had commissioned Cole Lesley to write a biography of Noël Coward. Known as Coley, Lesley had for many years been a lover of Coward's. Coward left him total access to his letters and his diaries, which meant this would be the 'official' book.

Coley lived in the Chalet Coward in Gstaad together with the actor Graham Payne, who had also been Coward's lover. While working on the book, Coley invited me to stay, and it turned out to be a most glamorous occasion. Once a year the Knie circus came to Gstaad and, as luck would have it, they were performing the weekend I was there. By tradition a very small group of close friends would mark the occasion by getting together and visiting the circus. Noël Coward had recently died and so this was the first outing without him. It was my good fortune to be included and I found myself at the circus sitting in a row alongside Prince Rainier of Monaco, Princess Grace, Charlie and Oona Chaplin, and of course Coley and Graham. At the end of the performance a pretty local girl presented Chaplin with an enormous bouquet of flowers, wrapped in cellophane. Very old and frail, and only just able to hold the bouquet, Charlie Chaplin raised it to his nose as if to smell the flowers. All eyes were on Charlie and then everyone in the circus tent stood up and cheered.

VANESSA REDGRAVE

We were offered Vanessa Redgrave's autobiography. It was not an auction but I was told that the outline would be sent simultaneously to four publishers. The combination of Vanessa's extraordinary acting talent, beauty and self-evident intelligence made this appear a most attractive proposition. We managed to agree terms and it was a book to which I especially looked forward. I asked to see some work in progress and a few months later Vanessa brought in eighty pages. We had what one might call 'a good meeting'.

On the following day I left for our house in France, taking Vanessa's manuscript with me. I recall it was a Wednesday and that the weekend thereafter happened to be Easter. The weather was sweltering and we decided to go to Saint-Tropez, which is horrendously crowded in the summer, but we did not think that Easter would present any problem without a hotel reservation. So, cheerfully, we set off and arrived in Saint-Tropez just after lunch with plenty of time to find a hotel. Or so we thought. We tried the four best. Full. We tried half a dozen cheaper hotels. Also full. At this point we acquired a list of B&Bs. Even among these not a room was to be found. Then I had an idea. I used to see a good deal of Tony Richardson (Vanessa's husband), one of our leading film and theatre directors. Tony had frequently said in his outgoing and generous way, 'You must come and stay with us at Le Garde Freinet.' There was just one snag: I had not seen Tony for ten years. None the less I was convinced he would welcome us and felt our dilemma justified giving him a call.

That was not as easy as it sounds. He was ex-directory and

no one in Saint-Tropez appeared to have his phone number. I suggested to Regina that we drive to Le Garde Freinet, where I was convinced we would obtain his phone number. Very reluctantly, Regina went along with my plan. She hates imposing on people and would have much preferred to drive back to our house in the Luberon. At Le Garde Freinet I made straight for the grocery store. By this time it was 7 p.m. but they were still open. They had the number and were willing to give it to me. I came out of the shop triumphant.

Now for the most difficult part. The call. I was lucky in that Tony answered the phone himself and immediately recognized my voice, which was surprising. I explained the circumstances and asked whether he could possibly put us up for the night. We would of course go out for dinner, I said. 'No question of that,' Tony declared. He welcomed us with open arms and absolutely insisted we stay for dinner. I had brought Vanessa's manuscript with me to read in Saint-Tropez, but something told me to leave it in the boot of the car.

The evening was an animated affair with various friends of Tony's as well as his and Vanessa's daughter Joely. The following morning we had an Easter breakfast and then we left to spend the day on the beach. From there, we returned to the Luberon and a day later to London. I had hardly set foot in my office when the phone rang. It was Vanessa's agent calling from Los Angeles. For me it was morning but for him it was night. 'What the fuck do you think you were doing checking up on Vanessa's book with Tony?' Presumably Joely had innocently mentioned my presence to her mother. Vanessa was furious and rang her agent. I called her immediately but nothing I said would persuade her of my innocence. A week later she had calmed down and we met, but she still did not believe my story and I can see that the coincidence was difficult to accept. Given the strength of her feelings, the only solution seemed to be to cancel the contract. And that is what we did.

A HOUSE IN THE LUBERON

REGINA AND I WERE on holiday driving around France. We were staying in a hotel just outside Joucas in the Luberon, when I went into the village to purchase some stamps and passed a house with a handwritten notice saying 'A Vendre' plus a telephone number. The thought of buying a house in France had never entered our minds but that evening I rang the number, simply out of curiosity, and discovered the price was 50,000 francs. 'That is five thousand pounds,' I told Regina excitedly.

'Just for fun', we decided to find out what else was on offer from a local estate agent. This is how we met an American lady called Gwen who proposed a house which was in ruins for three million francs (£300,000) and then another ruin for two and a half million francs. I told Gwen about the house in Joucas and she laughed, saying it was in the middle of the village and that it would cost a fortune to put right, and so on. We persisted until, on the second day, Gwen showed us a broken-down cottage complete with a well, a *pigeonnier* and three acres of vines for 250,000 francs. But there was a snag. Someone already had an option on it, although she did admit that this person had had the option for nine months. The house was called La Masure and we fell in love with it and, to our surprise, we wanted to buy it. Just like that. I proposed to the agent she give the potential buyer twenty-four hours to make up his mind and suggested I should ring her two days later, which I did. He had not come through, and we made a deal. La Masure was ours, a thrilling moment.

A year later our house was rebuilt and we were able to move in. It had just two bedrooms, a sitting room, a kitchen and a covered terrace looking out on to vines. Among our neighbours at the hamlet of Les Gros was Cameron Mackintosh, the impresario, who had recently put on *Les Misérables*, followed by *Phantom of the Opera*, followed by *Miss Saigon*. I recall Cameron pointing from our terrace to the bottom of the vineyard and saying, 'That is where the froggies live': it was his nickname for Boublil and Schonberg who had respectively written the lyrics and music for *Les Mis*, as Cameron referred to his staggeringly successful show. One day while we were having lunch together I asked Cameron who was publishing the book of *Les Mis*. It turned out that no one was, and so I made a contract on behalf of Cape.

We spent three happy years at La Masure. Our house was a thirty-minute walk from the village of Goult, which has the most attractive café in the region. Opposite the café was a branch of the Crédit Agricole, the 'Farmers' Bank'. We were told the bank was open half a day a week and so we joined. It turned out that they held no cash of any substance in stock and so if you wanted as much as, say, £500, you had to order it three days in advance. This is what I did. But when I called to collect the money I found sixteen farmers seated around the room. I went to the cash desk and was instructed to take my place on a seventeenth chair. I suspected that I might have to wait two or three hours. I could not help feeling that I had already earned the money in London and was disinclined to earn it again in Goult. I departed, but not before being told that the money would be returned to Avignon.

By this time Regina and I had come to adore the region. Whilst our house was the perfect summer home, it did not lend itself to life during the rest of the year, and so we decided to look for an alternative. By a stroke of good fortune we came across a *bastide* called Les Aspres, overlooking the high Luberon mountains, built in 1604 (you can hardly do better than that in our region), and with it came eighty acres of land. This was a paradise. Although we had not sold La Masure, we could not resist purchasing Les Aspres.

Between the house and an enormous flower garden there was a large stone courtyard. The only trees were two ancient *buis* (box trees). We built a round stone *bassin* and set it in a lawn. We planted some cedar trees and added a wide bed of white roses. They are called 'Iceberg' and flower almost constantly from May to December. Then we planted a wisteria against the south wall of the house. This flowers, miraculously, three times a year. The façade of the house was too beautiful to touch but we worked on the inside, repairing two marvellous vaulted rooms and creating a spectacular kitchen. Finally we built a terrace with pillars looking out on to the garden and the hillside beyond.

We had put La Masure on the market some six months previously, and at that time I mentioned our desire to move to Ed Victor. He told me that a client of his, Douglas Adams, the author of *The Hitchhiker's Guide to the Galaxy*, was living in Juan-les-Pins and looking for a house to buy in the South of France. 'Why not give him a ring?' said Ed. I knew Douglas slightly and I also knew how wealthy he was. I thought it inconceivable he would be the least bit interested in our place. A few months later I happened to see Ed again. He asked whether we had sold the house and I said, 'No,' explaining that we had meanwhile committed ourselves to another. Ed urged me even more strongly to get in touch with Douglas Adams. And so I did. He came over a few days later (Juan-les-Pins is about 150 miles from us and so 'coming over' is not nothing) with his wife and they looked around our house. He said he would like to return the following morning, which he did, and then he announced that he wanted to buy it. I did not argue about the price he offered because we wanted a quick exchange and that was fine by Douglas.

At this point a small nightmare began. Douglas (who had of course made an enormous amount of money from his books) brought in an army of advisers. One minute we were dealing with his solicitors (of which there were two, one English and one European). Then there was a financial adviser. And to top it all, there was a tax adviser. The completion date was delayed three times and I vowed that I would never speak to Douglas again. I didn't for several years. Finally I ran into him at a party in London and I asked the one question about which I had always been curious. 'When you came over from Juan-les-Pins, did you look at any other houses apart from ours?' Douglas said, 'No.' I find this bizarre but I believe it to be true.

In the South of France lives a writer whom I have published for many years and we have been the best of friends throughout those years. His name is Tom Wiseman, and he was the leading London showbiz columnist for the *Evening Standard* at a prodigiously early age, interviewing the stars from Deborah Kerr to Marlon Brando. Instead of the usual showbiz-flattering drivel, his column contained the truth as he saw it. Although he was feared for his frankness, it remained an accolade to be interviewed by him.

Then Tom decided to give up journalism, bought a house just outside Grasse, and determined to become a novelist. He wrote an historical novel about Hollywood called *Czar*. I did not like it at all, and, as is my way, I said so. Three years later he said he had written something altogether different and asked if I would consider it. The chances of my admiring his new book seemed extremely slim but of course I agreed to read it. The book was called *The Quick and the Dead* and, to my delight, I really admired it and offered a contract. This was followed by *The Romantic Englishwoman*, which was made into a film by Joseph Losey.

Tom, like most writers, is neurotic about the possible loss of a manuscript. When he went to England on one occasion, he deposited his new book at the bank in Nice for safekeeping. While in London he read a newspaper article with an account of a burglary at his bank during which the safe had been cracked. Tom's manuscript, wrapped in brown paper, was the one article the robbers left behind.

I owe a great personal debt to Tom and his wife Malou. It is this. They knew Regina from her years promoting films at the Cannes Film Festival. Her marriage was breaking up at the same time as mine and so Tom and Malou gave a small dinner in their London flat for us to meet. Regina disliked me on sight and I, for my part, totally ignored her. So much for that. I now come to the exceptional part. Five years later (and I do not exaggerate) the Wisemans tried again. And this time it 'took'.

We spent more than two years rebuilding Les Aspres. We stayed in a nearby hotel overseeing the works, and during that period we met a few people in the neighbourhood. I had mentioned to Abner Stein, the literary agent, the area in which we were living and he insisted we look up his friend and client Peter Mayle, who had just written a book about the region. Peter and his wife Jennie were most welcoming and invited us to lunch. We hit it off right away and Peter gave me a proof of his book, *A Year in Provence*, shortly to be published by Hamish Hamilton. I rang him a couple of days later to say how much I liked it. His publishers, he told me, were printing only 4,000 copies. I confessed that I would not have printed many more. The book did not take off immediately, but as the world knows, it went on to sell millions of copies. I recall an occasion not very long after publication when I was flying from London to Marseille (our nearest airport) and counted seven passengers reading Peter's book!

Our friendship with the Mayles grew and we loved to visit their cosy and happy home. Once, at Peter's house, we met Julian and Sheila More, a couple I knew and had particularly liked when I met them thirty years previously. Julian was the author of several successful musicals, including *Irma la Douce*. A few years later they had settled in France and now lived in Visan, about an hour's drive from us. On remeeting at the Mayles we literally fell into each other's arms at the joy of seeing one another and so unexpectedly after all these years.

As Peter's success grew and grew with *A Year in Provence* and the subsequent books, his happiness began to fade. He experienced a great deal of envy, especially from the English community, but also from some French local people. His loss of privacy became intolerable. Imagine, for example, a coachload of forty Japanese pulling up at your driveway, each of them clutching a copy of your book for signature, as well as the inevitable camera. Finally it became obvious to the Mayles, their love of Provence notwithstanding, that it was essential to move. And preferably far away. They chose Long Island in the United States, where they bought a beautiful house, and their new life appeared to have everything they wanted, except that it was not France, and not Provence. After three years they decided to sell and to return. And to do so as quietly and as secretively as possible.

By way of a PS, the French writer I most admired in my youth lived down the road from us at Lourmarin. I am referring to Albert Camus, the author of *The Fall* and *The Plague*. He was killed nearby in a car crash when he was on his way to Paris. The car was being driven by his publisher, Michel Gallimard, who also died in the crash.

THE DEAL

FOR A HOUSE primarily interested in books of quality our financial results were surprisingly good. In 1980 we made a profit of £800,000, which was phenomenal. And then our financial problems began. We started losing money, and we lost £100,000, £200,000, even more per year. We were co-owned by a small group that Graham had architected and included the Bodley Head and Chatto & Windus. Between the three of us we had a magnificent backlist and so we thought we were in a strong position to negotiate a merger with various publishing houses, notably Pan Macmillan and Penguin. The deals fell through and losses increased. By the autumn of 1986, Graham and I realized that we could not continue without additional capital. The obvious source was Max Reinhart, the chairman of the Bodley Head. He was our largest shareholder and was also wealthy. Max declined, believing we were going bust. The loan we required was £1,000,000. Graham talked to various banks and managed to raise the money. All that remained was for us to come up with the collateral. Graham and I agreed to go 50/50. My 'total worth', as they say, was £250,000 and so Graham gave a bank guarantee on my behalf for the balance. I was left with the interest to worry about, which came to far more than my gross salary. Graham did not seem the least bit worried, despite claiming to have no private income. I found the situation terrifying.

We continued to attempt to form various alliances but always came up against new obstacles. And so, for six months, I spent very many a sleepless night. I could see no way out. Graham was constantly optimistic, with City appointments that I rarely attended. Then one day in March 1987, I received a phone call from my friend Bob Gottlieb. He asked whether, if Si Newhouse were to fly over, we would be willing to talk to him.

Si Newhouse was the sixth richest man in America. He owned Condé Nast, *Vanity Fair*, the *New Yorker* and numerous newspapers and television stations. Most relevantly he also owned the Random House publishing group in America including the famous house of Knopf. I told Graham about the call and he was adamantly against the idea. Newhouse was American and there had been a long-term prejudice against American ownership. In addition, neither Graham nor I had even as much as considered selling. Our strategy had always been based on a determination to remain independent. I said that I felt strongly we should at least see Newhouse. In fact I said that we would be crazy *not* to see him. We were in a desperate situation, and surely we had nothing to lose. It appeared that Newhouse was inordinately keen and, in addition, he was reputed to be a civilized person, a man of good taste. Reluctantly Graham agreed. A date was fixed for two weeks hence. We were to meet for breakfast at the Connaught and keep the day open.

Breakfast was in Si's suite and we were still talking at 6 p.m. Si brought his lieutenant Bob Bernstein, but it was Si who did all the talking. He seemed incredibly knowledgeable about our backlist and deeply interested in how we ran the company. When we told him that we were not eager to sell he countered by talking of the perfect 'fit' with Random House, saying he was only interested in the best and clearly we were the best.

On two occasions Graham and I excused ourselves and walked around Hyde Park for half an hour or so. The first time was at about noon, the second mid-afternoon. It was obviously essential to talk to each other privately, and in addition, the fresh air was more than welcome. Graham's attitude was, roughly speaking: 'I told you this was a waste of time.' Mine was that I was intrigued and even impressed. Then came lunch and after lunch, the harder stuff. We had told Si we each earned £40,000. He said it was wrong to pay oneself so little and if he were able to make a deal he would insist on paying us double that. He asked about contracts. We said that we did not have any and did not want any. Si, on the other hand, attached a great deal of importance to them and felt they acted as a healthy protection for members of staff. He wanted us not just to have contracts, but long-term contracts. Would we accept ten years? Then we came to the crunch. It was casually thrown out: 'The price I offer you is twenty million pounds, to include the company's debts' (they came to four million). It happened so suddenly.

By now it was 4 p.m. and we were clearly due for another walk around the park. I knew, and Graham knew, that we had been offered more than double the value of the company. 'So what do you make of that?' I asked Graham. He was unmoved and uninterested. It was almost as though Si's offer had vindicated all of Graham's scepticism. Somehow I managed to win him over. At least a part of him must also have wanted the deal. And so, at the end of a single day, the unimaginable happened. We agreed to the deal and that it should be concluded as quickly as possible (within three weeks), since rumours could be damaging. We knew that Max Reinhart would be furious as this was a deal he had not engineered. However, we were not obliged to consult him. The fact that he had declined to put up the money we desperately needed had resulted in Graham and I holding over 50 per cent of the company between us, i.e. we were in control.

And this brings me to the sad part. We had our celebration dinner with the top people from both sides two weeks after that deal. Almost immediately thereafter, Si, or rather Bob Bernstein, informed Graham that whilst he was welcome to stay on, Simon Master (then at Pan) would be put in charge. Graham was shattered. He stayed on for a few weeks and then resigned. True, he received full financial compensation, but for him that was totally inadequate. In addition to feeling depressed on Graham's behalf I was extremely angry. I was convinced (and I remain convinced) that at the very moment Si was offering Graham a ten-year contract and telling us both how important it was that we should continue to run the company, he had already formulated his plan to appoint Simon Master. It is even possible that he had already offered Master the job subject only to his success in buying the company.

Occasionally I have expressed my disgust at Si's treatment of Graham. Doubling a man's salary and offering him a ten-year contract when you intend to replace him seems to me reprehensible. My friends who know far more than I do about the ways of the City tell me that I am being naïve. What Si did, they say, must be seen as no more than normal business practice.

It is hard to know how much happiness Si's purchase brought him. Clearly he was less than delighted with it for after ten years he sold his British holding, together with the Random House group in America, to Bertelsmann, a German company and the second largest publishing group in the world. Perhaps Si felt that we were not making enough money? Or perhaps he just got bored. Either way, for me the sale to Bertelsmann represented a betrayal.

TWO PAINTERS

DAVID HOCKNEY

I would like to have published many art books. But there were two publishers in England, Thames & Hudson and Phaidon, with a virtual monopoly in the field. This did not, however, prevent me from publishing a very few art books, and I am especially proud of two of them. The first was by a young and then totally unknown artist called David Hockney. The dealer who represented him, Kasmin, was a longstanding friend of mine. Our friendship dated back to the mid-fifties. I recall going to an exhibition Kasmin had put on which I think was Hockney's first, and it was in 1958. Only drawings were on show and I was so impressed that I bought a line drawing as well as two prints. I remember hesitating over the drawing which seemed so expensive. It cost £8. Today it must be worth £25,000.

I told Kasmin the drawings reminded me a little of Matisse and I thought them so wonderful I wanted to publish a book of them. Needless to say, publishing a completely unknown artist is risky, but none the less we chose a stylish format and called the book simply *72 Drawings*. It did not occur to me that this little book might sell well, and indeed sales were slow to begin with, but within a few years we had sold close to 100,000 copies. David was delighted and as a result of our publication I got to know him somewhat. Famous for his Yorkshire sense of humour, he is ever ready to send up others for taking themselves too seriously and he is equally ready to make fun of himself. At the same time he is always willing to talk seriously about art, and he does so with no pretension at all.

In those days Kasmin had a house in the Dordogne. He invited me to stay while David was there and also the dress designer Ossie Clarke. Each morning Kas (as Kasmin is called) went to the local market, coming back with aubergines, peppers and enormous tomatoes. These he would put before David, knowing that each drawing would be worth a very great deal. It rained and it rained and it rained, as it often does in the Dordogne. After four days of rain David took off in his car. He had only been gone some two hours when he rang to tell us that the sun was shining brilliantly a little further south and he suggested we should all join him.

LUCIAN FREUD

The other artist I published was Lucian Freud and very far from being any kind of discovery of mine. Most would agree that he is the greatest living English painter. He is certainly the most expensive. The volume we published was the 'definitive' art book of his work, 360 pages, all in colour and in an enormous format. The book is beautifully designed and beautifully produced. Our publishing it came about, as is so often the case, in a roundabout way. I had, in collaboration with Mark Holborn, who is in charge of picture books for Cape, commissioned the arts journalist Bruce Bernard to write a book about the Soho School, including Freud of course. Bernard's rate of progress over a period of a year was almost nil and so, given the fact that he was a close friend of Freud (who incidentally painted a portrait of him), I suggested to Mark that we might, all three of us together, approach Freud for a definitive book. The reason for going via Bruce was that Freud is reputed to be suspicious, if not difficult. It turned out that the idea of being published by a general publisher, rather than an art publisher, appealed to him. Furthermore, he knew just how expensive it is to produce a beautiful art book and instructed his lawyers to take this into account when negotiating the contract.

I cannot say that I got to know Freud during the publishing process. For me the most rewarding aspect was in the selection of the pictures and the correction of proofs. We had three joint sessions at the studio of the designer Derek Birdsell. Mark and I always turned up together and Freud would be waiting for us, his presence clearly signalled by the Bentley, invariably illegally parked on the pavement just outside the studio. For the first session Freud invited his friend Frank Auerbach in order to have an additional professional eye. It was fascinating to watch Freud move around the long tables where the pictures were laid out, darting about as if he were stalking the paintings. It was a question of the order and of the pairing of the pictures. At the first session, I did not say a word. By the second I ventured to make a contribution. Once, or perhaps even twice, Freud agreed with something I had said, which seemed like an enormous accolade.

From time to time we would take a break and on one occasion I heard Freud mention, quite casually, that he had been giving a series of taped interviews to William Feaver, the art critic of the *Observer*. I gathered the interviews were comprehensive and frank and it amazed me that Freud had done such a thing, for he is famously secretive. I mentioned it to Mark, as clearly a book of such interviews would be of enormous interest.

When the manuscript was complete and Freud had read it, he decided, unsurprisingly, against publication. Mark asked if he might none the less read the book 'in confidence', but in vain. When it came to a publication party for the art book at Derek's studio everyone connected with the book was present with just one exception – Lucian Freud.

PHOTOGRAPHERS

HENRI CARTIER-BRESSON

The first book of photographs I published was by Henri Cartier-Bresson. Not a bad beginning. Many would consider him to be the greatest photographer of our time. He was an extremely private man and went to great lengths to avoid being photographed himself. This is in no way connected with my having published him, but it so happens that Henri took some pictures of me, aged twenty, and I still possess a print. It came about by chance. He was very fond of my then girlfriend, Martha Crewe, and he happened to be visiting her Notting Hill Gate home when I dropped in. To my amazement he took out his camera and that was that. It was by all accounts, a most unusual thing for him to do. Many, many years later, to celebrate my son Ben's twenty-first birthday, my ex-wife, Fay, got in touch with Henri to ask whether she could purchase a print of the picture he had taken of me forty years previously. To my amazement he was able to lay his hands on the negative and Ben now possesses a signed print of the photograph. Imagine how orderly his archive must be. I have observed that such order appears to be characteristic of photographers.

A Cartier-Bresson story which is engraved on my mind goes back a number of years. I was alone in a Paris café, having a *grande crème*. Cartier-Bresson was at a table nearby, talking

Quentin Blake
after Henri Cartier-Bresson

to a young lady, his camera uncharacteristically on the table. I went over to him to say hello. He ignored me. I told him my name and he continued to look blank. Then I mentioned Martha's name, but to no avail. He absolutely refused to respond. Non-recognition of this kind can make one feel terrible. I even wondered whether, perhaps, I had made a mistake, but I am certain that it was he at the other table. Henri and his wife lived in a converted farmhouse at Cereste, some twenty miles from the house we bought in the Luberon. One day I rang them and fortunately Martine answered the phone. She knew exactly who I was (by this time I had published Henri's book) and she invited me and my daughter Hannah to lunch. It was a casual and altogether happy occasion. Henri was surprisingly welcoming. Of course I did not mention the Paris encounter! He talked about having given up photography in favour of watercolours. He was so excited at this new course of events.

DON McCULLIN

I have a much more straightforward relationship with Don McCullin, the leading British war photographer. I published his autobiography, a marvellous account of his life and works. Don makes photographs of warfare (mainly Vietnam) in all its horror, meaningful and even beautiful. In 1989 he produced *Open Skies*, a book on the countryside surrounding his house in Dorset. Thus he went from one extreme to the other, but whatever the subject matter his work retains a comparable power.

Don often comes to London and on one occasion Regina and I had invited him to dinner. The evening turned out to be strangely memorable. Don arrived somewhat late with his arm in a sling and his face badly bruised. He excused himself profusely and did not require much persuasion to offer an explanation. It appeared that he'd discovered that the fashion photographer Terry O'Neill (a good friend of his) had been taking out his girlfriend. He was so angered by this that he went round to Terry's house to have the matter out with him. When he arrived O'Neill was not at home and the maid did not know when to expect him. Don insisted on sitting down on a sofa and announced that he would wait for O'Neill, however long it took. As soon as Terry turned up, Don went for him and then he came on to us for dinner. He assured us that O'Neill was in far worse condition than he.

DAVID DOUGLAS DUNCAN

David Douglas Duncan, another great war photographer, worked originally for *Life* magazine. When he came to live in the South of France he bought a house in a place called Castelaras and it was there that he and his wife, Sheila, got to know Regina. It was also there that he met Picasso, who lived nearby. David grew close to him and as a result of their friendship he published a number of Picasso-related books, *Picasso's Women*, *Picasso's Poetry*, *Goodbye Picasso*. He brought photographs from these books to show me at the Frankfurt Book Fair on several occasions, but for one reason or another I declined to publish any of them. He was always philosophical and courteous.

LARTIGUE

In the South of France, near the Duncans' home, lives another close friend of Regina. On one occasion she invited us to a lunch party at her house and there I met the man who is my favourite photographer of all time: Lartigue. I am not saying he is the greatest of all photographers (though I would certainly rank him as one of them) but his work delights me more than any other. There is such motion, such directness and such joy in his pictures. He loved especially to photograph children and in this respect had a gift which was unique. I had always hoped that I might meet him one day and by the time I did he was already well into his eighties. I was literally overwhelmed at being in the presence of my idol. We got talking and he mentioned that these days he had taken up oil painting, and he invited us to come and see the pictures the following day. Of course we accepted. When we got there his wife, a good deal younger than Lartigue, climbed up into the loft and handed the pictures down for him to present to us. Alas, I thought the paintings really bad. But there is no point in lamenting this when it was so clear that the act of painting gave him enormous pleasure.

RICHARD AVEDON

I will end this section with another great photographer, but great in a rather different field. This is Richard Avedon. We signed a multiple contract with him, multiple because he had an enormous amount of work to be published, multiple also because his agent happens to be Andrew Wylie. The books were to appear under the Cape imprint and it was Mark Holborn who was responsible for the acquisition. Avedon is perhaps best known for his fashion photography. Many of his other pictures, especially his portraits, are equally important. For the publication of our first book, we put on an exhibition together with the National Portrait Gallery and held a party for the opening. Alongside this was a second, tiny drinks gathering for just a dozen people. One of them was Princess

Diana. It so happened that my mother-in-law, Lydia, was in London at the time and she came with us. Lydia, who is of Russian origin, speaks little English, but she made eye contact with Diana, greeting her by making circular movements with the palm of her right hand. Princess Diana returned the gesture in exactly the same way and gave that magical smile of hers. It is a moment Lydia will not forget, and I must confess that I shall not either.

COOKBOOKS

MADHUR JAFFREY

Food has always been an important part of my life. My mother was a particularly good cook, though she never used a recipe book. My first wife, Fay, loved to cook and became a famous restaurant critic, and my second wife is quite simply a superb cook. Given this, one might imagine I would have built up a strong cookery list. But this did not happen, although I have derived a special pleasure from publishing a select few cookbooks.

One of them, and only one, was something of a discovery. It was *An Invitation to Indian Cookery* by the actress Madhur Jaffrey. She played in *Shakespeare Wallah* and then she wrote her first book. This was closely followed by a second, *Indian Vegetarian Cooking*. Usually a cook is fortunate to find two or three desirable recipes in any one book, but in the case of Madhur Jaffrey there are many, and in addition she writes beautifully.

While I am proud of the small part I played as her publisher, the credit must go to Judith Jones, who was the Knopf cookery book editor, for it was she who brought Madhur to my attention. I also owe to Judith the fact that we came to publish *From Julia Child's Kitchen*. Julia Child is one of the great names in America, where her books have sold hundreds of thousands of copies. This stems, in part, from her numerous appearances on television. In England, by contrast, we sold disgracefully few copies of her book. Julia is also co-author with Simone Beck of *Mastering the Art of French Cooking*, which is one of the cookbook classics. Alas, we did not publish it.

MRS BEETON'S COOKBOOK

We did, however, publish *Mrs Beeton's Book of Household Management*, the great Victorian classic. This came about in rather an unusual way. On a journey to Wales I stopped in the town of Ross-on-Wye. It was market day and there on a bookstall I found an ancient copy of *Mrs Beeton* which I bought for 20p. When I arrived at my cottage in the Black Mountains I leafed through the book and found many traditional recipes, traditional with a difference. Quantities would, for example, relate to buying a whole pig rather than 4lb of pork. Then there were recipes of a different nature, such as instructions on how to make boot polish. The book went on to detail the handling of staff, including the invaluable piece of information that 'the mistress is the general of the household'. As a piece of social history it was riveting. I turned to the front and discovered that I had bought a second edition. It occurred to me that a facsimile of the first edition could be very successful.

Back at the office, we advertised for a first edition and managed to find one, at a cost 500 times greater than the sum I had paid for my copy. Even today *Mrs Beeton* remains the most famous English cookbook of all time. I was convinced that by this time the entire book would be out of copyright, but to make sure we were in the clear I sent the book to our lawyer, Michael Rubinstein, who confirmed it was safe to

reproduce the original. We were determined, naturally, that our edition should be a genuine facsimile. The book had well over 1,000 pages, but we did not regard the length as a problem, for we were convinced that we would sell a great number of copies. The only complication was to find a way to reproduce the colour plates, but this we managed.

As publication day approached my conscience began to trouble me. We were in the process of publishing a prodigiously famous book which was, after more than 100 years, still very much in print with another publisher. I wrote to Ward Lock (*Mrs Beeton's* publisher from the beginning) and told them of our project, offering to pay a small royalty (2.5 per cent). Back came an outraged letter from the Chairman demanding we abandon our plan, at which point I took a delight in withdrawing my offer.

Our publication received enormous coverage. Reviewers had never seen an early edition and were as fascinated as I had been. We sold close to 100,000 copies of the hardcover and a further 200,000 of a paperback edition in the same format. Bearing in mind that we were not paying any author's royalties, this became a colossally profitable venture. I took a copy of the book with me to the Frankfurt Book Fair. The first publisher I ran into there was Roger Straus of Farrar, Straus. I showed him my fat little volume and he was enchanted. He bought the American rights on the spot. Surprisingly for something so intrinsically English, the book became a bestseller in America also.

PAMELA HARLECH

I suspect that I came to publish *Harlech's Feast* because of the author's personality. Pamela Harlech was a food writer for *Vogue* and also a well-known social figure, married to Lord Harlech of Harlech Television. The book, as one would expect from its title, was made up of rather elaborate recipes. When we had put the collection together Pam decided to celebrate with a small dinner party. There were just six of us: Harold Macmillan, Princess Margaret, a man from *Vogue*, the Harlechs and me. I had never met either Macmillan or Princess Margaret and was, naturally, curious about both of them.

We were standing about having drinks before dinner when Princess Margaret sat down upon an enormous sofa. Everyone else seemed suddenly to have disappeared and I was faced with the choice of disappearing also or sitting down beside Princess Margaret on the sofa. I chose the latter. She wanted to know what I did and I told her I was a publisher. Her comment was: 'Oh, but books are *so* expensive.' We talked some more and meanwhile I wondered which book I should send her. The following day, at my office, I decided upon *The French Lieutenant's Woman* and I received a five-page handwritten letter of thanks. Princess Margaret was perceptive about the book and in addition she was enormously grateful for the gift.

We sat down to dinner, where I found myself mesmerized by Macmillan, not so much for what he said as for his immobile face. He looked like a poker player. Shrewd, and at pains to give nothing away. I felt that one would be in relatively safe hands with such a man as Prime Minister. Princess Margaret's conduct during dinner was extraordinary. She addressed most of what she had to say to the man from *Vogue* and I had the feeling he had been invited for her. Her subject for the evening was Tony Snowdon. I had heard that they were not getting on by this time. But I had no idea of the degree to which she hated him. And, even less, of the degree to which she would hold forth about him to strangers. I can think of no more relevant word than that she was vituperative about him as a husband, as a man, and as a father.

A NEAR THING

DURING MY FORTY YEARS at Cape there were two occasions on which my job was seriously in jeopardy. The first, as I have already said, was in 1961; the second crisis occurred twenty-seven years later in the summer of 1988. That spring I had grown ever-increasingly depressed. It was called a clinical depression and simply came over me. No one could offer any explanation. My doctor suggested I take a sabbatical of three months or so. Shortly before I left, a new Managing Director was appointed. At that point I was still Chairman and had been so for some twenty years. The new man was called Bing Taylor, and he was taken on by Simon Master. When I departed for my sabbatical in France he had not yet started working at Cape. I met with him, however, and made one specific request: he should not move into my office. This was not primarily for my sake, but I wanted my colleagues at Cape to feel reassured that my absence was only temporary. Bing said he 'would not dream of' using my office. I discovered shortly after I left for France that he had installed himself in it. I decided to say nothing at that point.

By mid-July, though still feeling low, I thought it time to discuss the future and got in touch with Simon Master. He informed me that Bing was to run the company and chair all important meetings, including the editorial meeting, which had been my most precious domain. Simon wrote me a long letter, a letter I have kept. He said the triumph of Cape was embodied in my genius (yes, that was the word he used) but this was also something of an Achilles heel. He went on to say that they very much wanted me back at Cape and this applied to my authors as much as my colleagues. His statement outraged me, for as far as I knew there had never been any question of my *not* returning. I replied, answering his letter point by point. Some three weeks before the due date of my return, by which time I was feeling a new man, I rang Simon. I told him that I had learned Bing was in my office and I said that unless Simon moved him out, I would not return. The rest, including Bing's role, could await discussion when and if I returned. To my amazement Bing was no longer with us when I returned.

During my sabbatical I received a large number of wonderful letters. Some have got lost in the intervening years but I will quote a few of the most remarkable. I do so not out of vanity, but because the letters became a part of my life alongside the condition in which I found myself. The degree of caring shown by my authors was immensely flattering, even elating. The most generous of all was Roald Dahl. I have already mentioned that his letter was nine long handwritten pages, and must have taken him a whole day or even two to write. Roald's letter is so wonderful that I will quote from it at considerable length, and you will observe that his main purpose was to entertain rather than to inform me. I felt enormously cherished.

11 August 1988   *Gipsy House*

Dear Tom,
    Your letter arrived two hours ago and I was awfully pleased to hear from you. I am going to write you a nice long reply with any news that may interest you.
    Liccy (note sp.) and I are very well. Five of our seven

children are presently in the United States, in Florida, California, Boston, Martha's Vineyard, etc. Here we have only Theo and one of Liccy's (Lorna), so things are comparatively quiet. Our lovely full-time gardener died suddenly of a stroke six weeks ago, so now we are both working outdoors to keep things looking good. Yesterday afternoon I was smothered in a forest of raspberry canes, thinning out the old wood, and suddenly an American voice nearby said, 'Hello, Mr Dahl, I'm from New Jersey. I've come down to see you.' I peered out and there was a pleasant-looking fair-haired youth smiling shyly. Usually I show them politely to the door but this time I talked to him for an hour while I went on with my raspberry work. I'm afraid this house is becoming a place of pilgrimage. The day before, I was eating my lettuce and ham for lunch alone (Liccy in London) and I saw through the window three people, two women and a youth, walking up and down the lane. Finally I went out and asked if they were lost. 'No, no! Vee are from Holland. Vee haff come to look at your house.' Then out came the cameras and in went me. Every day parents drive children in cars up the lane and get out at the top car park and stare and stare. I suppose I should be pleased and I do try not to be snappy to them all, but it gets a bit much at times. So how is Cape from my point of view now? About 5 weeks ago I passed the word via Murray that I had no one there to talk to anymore. Nobody had told me anything apart from a note from Bing Taylor announcing his appointment. After all, I had a new book [Revolting Rhymes 2] to talk to them about. Should it be for children or for adults? The upshot was a series of messages via Murray inviting Liccy and I plus Murray and Gina to dinner with Simon Master and Bing at the Connaught. A date was finally set and we went to dinner. I had never met Simon before. I knew Bing only from the old 'Good Book Guide days' and I had liked him. In fact I had helped him in the very early times taking him round and introducing him to various publishers like Alan Brooke and Kaye Webb. So we dined and they were very pleasant. 'But look here,' I said, 'who do I talk to in future about my books?' Simon pointed to Bing, and Bing said, 'Me.' I said, 'OK, but you might have told me before.'

I don't think I have spoken to either of them since, so you can see why I am glad you are coming back. They are not very 'approachable' people. Simon is immersed in sums and policy and Bing, I presume, is learning what publishing is all about. Don't get me wrong, nice fellows, both of them but no glow exudes from them and precious little enthusiasm. So since you have been away, my mentor and phone-talker has been Liz Attenborough. She is a good egg, she chats, she laughs, she is right on the ball. I like her. And she has gradually moulded a very efficient department around her both for marketing and for publicity. Primarily because of Liz, I recently accepted an invitation to go to Australia next March/April ostensibly to open the Adelaide festival of arts. But of course we will be doing Penguin/Puffin work mostly in Sydney, Adelaide and Perth. We will travel slowly and in as much comfort as possible, perhaps via Los Angeles outward, and via Singapore returning. I will be 72 in September. I tire quickly. I hate time changes, but Australia has been very good to me and I want to try to pay them back a little. Talking of Australia, their schools are not on holiday like ours in June, July, August. So all my fan mail during these months comes from there. But my secretary is on holiday and has been for three weeks. So the Australian mail, primarily from schools, has piled up something stupendous. About 1,500 letters in large envelopes. Last week Liccy put the whole lot in a huge sort of laundry basket in my secretary's room. Theo, who burns all the waste paper baskets in the house, thought they were junk and burnt the lot. Rather than having half the school teachers and children in Australia think I was an off-hand bugger like Le Carré who replies to nothing I wrote a little piece addressed to Australian schools telling exactly what had happened and apologizing for not replying to their letters. This went to Liz Attenborough who faxed it to Penguin HQ in Melbourne and from there it went on the wire service to all national newspapers. I think it saved my face and saved my secretary, incidentally, a great deal of work.

Valerie K phoned me yesterday with the sad news that she is retiring at the end of the month (but will be back to see you on September 5th). We had a good chat. She is a nice woman.

Then she phoned me again at 4 p.m. 'I must call once more,' she said, 'because I have just seen the sales figures of Matilda, *they are going up each week rather than down. Last week we sent out 4,500 copies, the total will soon reach a hundred thousand.'*

More about Matilda. *The Redgrave theatre company who put on Adrian Mole to run in the West End for fifteen months as a play with incidental music (it's now running in 15 other countries) are going to do* Matilda *as a fully fledged musical comedy! Four nice intelligent men came down here to lunch last week – the director, the scriptwriter and two composers – to talk about it all. They are mad keen and they have got the money to do it. Rather fun.*

There is so much going on in the film world with the children's books I can't keep up with it.

1) The BFG, full animation, soon ready.

2) The Witches, Jim Henderson, directed by Nick Roeg, a full-length feature. Mai Zetterling (the grandmother), Anjelica Houston (the Grand High Witch). The shooting is now finished. Cutting and music will be completed by end November. I saw some rushes last week. It's pretty scary stuff. Budget thirteen and a half million!

3) Danny the Champ of the World. Full-length feature, starts shooting on September 4th near Henley. Already one thousand pheasants have been bought. The script is wonderful. Absolutely true to the book. Here's the interesting thing about this one. It has big stars. Jeremy Irons plays Danny's father, his own son plays Danny. Alan Bates plays Jim Hassell the nouveau-riche land owner. Jeremy Irons' wife (Sinead Cusack) plays the vicar's wife. Sinead Cusack's father, Cyril Cusack, plays the doctor. This could be a very good film.

4) The Wonderful Story of Henry Sugar is being shot in Rome but in English, of course, by an Italian producer who came to London to see me a couple of weeks ago. I liked him.

5) What else. Countless video films for children seem to be being made of all the children's books, something they call animatic video, which tells the story with still colour pictures. This apparently does not impinge on the ordinary film rights.

And it seems to me that straight tapes of every book, read either by me or by actors, are used by all parents to keep their offspring quiet during car journeys and also for sending them to sleep at night.

I am not quite sure I want to write anything else. Each new book only adds to the general turmoil in this house. There are now 17 children's books. When Revolting Rhymes 2 comes out it will be 18 and as you know, these little books are not like adult books by say Fowles or Burgess. They go on and on. They even seem to gather momentum each year in paperback, so every new one simply adds to the accumulation and I get more and more boggled. Yes, I think I'll take a break. A very long break. Ten days ago Liccy had a bright idea. 'Why,' she said, 'don't you and Quentin do a Christmas card for the Great Ormond Street

Wishing-well fund?' So I called Quent. He said yes at once.
I called Great Ormond Street. They were ecstatic. I called
Penguin. They are getting one of their big printers, probably
Hazel Watson and Viney, to print them free. Next I had to
write a little verse. So this was it:

WHERE ART THOU MOTHER CHRISTMAS?

> Where art thou, Mother Christmas?
> I only wish I knew
> Why Father should get all the praise
> And no one mentions you.
>
> I'll bet you buy the presents
> And wrap them large and small
> While all the time that rotten swine
> Pretends he's done it all.
>
> So Hail to Mother Christmas
> Who shoulders all the work!
> And down with Father Christmas,
> That unmitigated jerk!

Quentin is doing the picture of Mother Christmas right now.
There was a meeting between Puffin and Great Ormond
Street at which it was decided they could easily sell 750,000
cards. All Penguin reps will be used to distribute to
bookshops throughout UK. Each bookshop order form will
have a number and at the end there will be a draw (just to
chivvy the bookshops) and the winning bookshop will get a
signing session from me, wherever it may be. I am told the
card itself will make a lot of money for the hospital. Several
hundred thousand. It's good.

Kenneth Baker, the Secretary of State for Education,
came up to me some months ago and asked me to go on his
high powered committee which will decide precisely what
and how English is taught in schools for the next decade.
I said no. He said yes. I said no again. He said please.

So I said yes. I attended the first meeting. Twelve people,
nearly all professors, academics. I sat there for 4 hours.
I made a few remarks that I considered sensible. They
ignored them. A week later, I wrote to the Sec. of State
saying, I am not a committee man. I have worked all my
life alone. I cannot function en masse. I resign. He wrote
back a lovely handwritten letter saying he understood. 'You
have already done more than enough in teaching children
English, etc. etc.' So that was that.

But listen Tom. Will you be able to function properly
alongside all these Bings and Simons when you come back?
I had the feeling that some kind of entrenchment was going
on in your absence, even to make it difficult for you to slide
back into your proper place again. Mind you, I do agree that
you should do a lot less this time around, and if these other
chaps are willing to take some of the burden off you and
at the same time give you a free hand as before, then it all
might work very well. I cannot see you being pushed around
though by anyone. I so hope it will all work out. Make it.

From the other letters sent to me, I have selected a few by
two of my favourite authors. The first of these is Doris Lessing.
Her style moves me. I love the way the words flow and the
way she *cares*. I quote the following:

25 May 1988

My dear Tom,
*   I hope all that follows is not what you know already, but*
I have been seeing Bob Ornstein, who is a bit of an expert
on things of the mind. He suggests that you should look
particularly at two areas.
*   1. Possible allergies. He says that it is common for people*
*   to develop allergies in their fifties and often for things*
*   they have been eating all their lives. (I have always*

*eaten roast beef and it has never done any harm.) You
can test yourself for allergies by giving up something
for a week and seeing if it makes you better. Common
ones: wheat products, milk products, certain fruits, etc.*
2. *Deficiencies. You can get yourself tested for
deficiencies. Often a cause of depression.*

*There is a doctor called Davis, well known in this field.
He cured my friend G. of depressions. He used to have
terrible depressions. G. is now on a pretty strict diet, vitamin
supplements, etc. Davis is booked up for some time ahead.
You could make a date now for when you get back. At least
it won't do any harm.*

*Bob says exercise is extremely important for depressives.
A hard session of walking or something every day.*

Much love to you and to Regina.
    Doris

                                          19 July 1988

Dearest Tom,

*Your letter was dated 22 June, nearly a month ago –
I would have written at once, but I have just come back
from Houston.*

*And of course your letter made me sad, you sound so low
and unlike Tom. I know you'll get better, people do, I've
known other people who get 'depressed' – a silly label word
for such an affliction. But just as it descends, apparently
without reason, so it goes away. I've come to believe that
locked inside 'depression' is a mine of energy, I've seen how a
depressed person comes out of it, transformed, as if, within the
'depression' all kinds of transformations were going on . . . but
I am babbling. I do know very well that to someone inside
that truthful painful state, people outside can seem very trivial
and thoughtless. I remember sitting with Jenny, who was in
the depths, and making all kinds of consoling 'helpful'
remarks, and seeing in her eyes how facile I seemed to her.*

*The opera was a great success in Houston, standing
ovations and all that, but Houston is not London, cool and
sophisticated London. We'll see. London will have the benefit
of Houston's mistakes, changes will be made, it will be better
here in many ways, but one: the two lead singers in Houston
sweated blood to get their roles right, and cared so much
about it, I can't believe succeeding singers will be able to
project so much warmth and tenderness. I hope you'll be here
in early November and that you and Regina will be my
guests that first night.*

*I enjoyed working there so much: I don't think anything
has ever been so much fun. And then, of course, I live a pretty
isolated life and it is nice to get into a group of people,
working.*

*I am sitting here surrounded by the usual chaos of letters I
have to write, nearly all of them boring.*

I wonder when you are coming back? Not yet, I expect.

*I shall be here as far as I know till autumn, at least. Look
after yourself, dear Tom. I am thinking of you and wishing
you well.*

Give my love to Regina. Much love.
Doris

My other special favourite author is Kurt Vonnegut. He
writes with a sense of humour and imagination and with a
gusto quite unlike anyone else.

Dear Tom,

*It was brought to my attention yesterday that you have
been experiencing deep depressions. I know a lot about those,
and about unhappy marriages as well. I write now to assure
you that I love you, and that we who do are numerous and
concerned.*

*I have benefited lavishly from the high you were able to
sustain for nearly half a century. The longest high I ever had*

was two weeks right at the end of the Second World War. For what it may be worth, here is what I have found out about highs and lows over the years: they only seem to be connected with what is really going on. They are actually no more synchronized with our adventures than are sunshine and thunderstorms.

They are chemicals.

Ask my son Mark.

There are many great days in the midst of the deepest depressions, during which I say to myself, 'My God . . . what on earth was the matter with me yesterday?'

Again my love

Kurt

Dear Tom!

Happy Birthday, good old pal. Damned if we haven't stuck together through thick and thin.

I've written a preface for a new edition of Slaughterhouse-5 in which I note Stephen Hawking's mystification about why we can't remember the future. I say that we merely have to grow old in order to discover what will become of ourselves and our families and our friends and enemies. Without resort to a crystal ball or tarot cards I now know that you will indeed become England's most perceptive and courageous and supportive publisher of books, and that you will sleep each night in the arms of a wise and beautiful woman who adores you.

Not bad.

After you and I visited my neighbour Bob Dash, a painter and famous gardener, you asked me if I, like you, didn't come on some with attractive persons of the gay persuasion. Please find me shamelessly flirtatious with you today.

Love as always.

Kurt

Dear Tom,

    It's an honor to hear from you always, but particularly one when you have come through a period of such terrible and pointless and inexplicable testing. Thank goodness for Regina. Most of us have to do without such unflagging support and sympathy, which we probably don't deserve. I must have told you before that the University of Iowa Medical Center made a study of the afflictions peculiar to writers, and discovered that we are all depressives from families of depressives. You are one of us. A misfortune. Critics who have never heard of Marquez belonging to a very different and presumably more steadily cheerful branch of the human race.

    Several months back a lady from the TLS, although an American, interviewed me in Manhattan, as arranged for by your publicity people. She found me a very strange person, not at all what she had expected, she said. She asked me finally if I knew I was eccentric. Did she publish anything which would indicate why she found me so batty? The mention of Marquez put me in mind of her. At one point she asked me what I thought of this author or that one, including Woody Allen and Tom Wolfe, and I said that when you come to the big city you have to expect to run into Mozart. Marquez is really Mozart, but I would not be sorry to run into him. When I finally met Mohammed Ali, I was happy to swoon with admiration. I would do the same for Marquez. There is the barest chance that I did once meet him when not even writers had noticed him. Would you ask him if he was at the P.E.N. Congress in Stockholm in about 1974 or so?

    I think you can trust the feeling that you will never be hit by depression so hard again. My son Mark, a world class depressive with three hashmarks for visits to the bughouse, finally understands that he will be OK as long as he keeps away from stimulants of any kind. He is a stalwart in

Alcoholics Anonymous, as is Edith and one of my adopted Adams kids.

Which reminds me of a conversation we had one time about the fact that the Adams kids, my wards, had a grandmother on the Adams side who was Jewish, but who became an Episcopalian, and who thereafter denied her Jewishness. You suggested that I blow her cover. Out of respect for her strong feelings in this matter, which I do not admire, I never have. I probably will some day, causing mild surprise and little more. I have a cousin who is a sweet nut on genealogy, and I asked him if I had any Jewish ancestors, and he said that indeed I had: one of my sixty-four great-great-great-great-grandparents was a Jew named Rienermann in Munster, a convert to Catholicism who became the Court Painter in Westphalia. Now here I am denying that I am either a Christian or a Jew or anything.

Love as always.
Kurt

Dear Tom,

In 6 more days I shall be 60. I was talking to Norman Mailer a while back, about getting old, and I said to him, 'Soon it will be Festschrift time.' Jill asked me the meaning of the word, and now, thanks to her, I am about to receive a Festschrift. She now knows two words in German. 'Gesundheit' is what you say when somebody sneezes, and 'Festschrift' is what you say when somebody turns 60 years old.

I am cooperating with Nigel Finch of BBC, although I might be wise to be wary of him. He seems keen on showing how crazy or foolish Americans are. We'll see. I guess he will come with a camera crew in a couple of weeks. As for Jill's and my visit to England in February, I have penciled it in, but am a little worried about how much singing I am expected to do for our suppers. We intend to do the trip

stylishly, coming on the Concorde and staying at a really
spiffy hotel. I certainly don't expect you and Panther to pay
for all of it. If you will give us enough for ordinary travel,
I will of course pay all the surcharges. It will be a sort of
honeymoon, since we have never had one. But it will be
no honeymoon at all if I am, as has been suggested by your
promotional expert, to be delivering public lectures all the
time. I do very little public speaking over here, you know,
although I have sometimes been offered enormous fees to do
so. I suppose I would be speaking for glory over there. If I
really do that, I will have to write something appropriate.
I have no standard vaudeville performance sure to please.
In the past, I've gone on TV and radio shows, usually in the
daytime or early evening, and have had plenty of time for
theatre and restaurants. Mightn't I do that again? I want
you to be happy, but I want my wife to be happy too.
Advise.

    Yours truly
    Kurt

P.S. My daughter Edith is in love with a lumberjack, and
painting better than ever.

I will conclude by mentioning, in no particular order, the names of some of the authors who wrote me some kind and generous letters in the summer of 1988. They are: Nadine Gordimer, Martin Amis, Harold Evans, Ralph Steadman, Brian Moore, Quentin Blake, Anita Brookner, Heathcote Williams, Julian Barnes, John Fowles, Zandra Rhodes, Bernard Levin, John Irvin, Salman Rushdie and Bruce Chatwin.

THE FRANKFURT BOOK FAIR

THE FRANKFURT BOOK FAIR, by far the biggest in the world, began as a showcase for German publishers to display their wares to German booksellers. Gradually it became increasingly international and today it is so large that it would take a week simply to walk all the way around it. The booksellers have virtually dropped out and the main purpose of the fair has become the selling and the buying of rights, with each publishing house renting a booth according to its size. I have attended this jamboree for thirty-five years in a row and like many other publishers have developed a love–hate relationship with it. In my case, a part of this relates to the fact that the fair takes place in Frankfurt so that if I wish to attend, I am obliged to go to Germany. Nothing else would induce me to do so.

Traditionally my first port of call was the Italian stand of Feltrinelli. There, if I was lucky, I would find both Giangiacomo and his wife Inge. The Feltrinelli firm has had a dramatic history. Giangiacomo was one of the wealthiest men in Italy. He was also a Communist and began publishing primarily in order to make left-wing texts he considered important available to students. Within a couple of years he had acquired world rights in Pasternak's *Dr Zhivago* and in *The Leopard* by Lampedusa. To say these two books put his publishing house on the map is an understatement. Some years later Giangiacomo was assassinated and his body found at the foot of an electricity pole. The reason remains a mystery. After his death the ebullient, generous and adorable Inge took over and she has, along with her son Carlo, been at the helm ever since. She also runs the flourishing and impressive Feltrinelli bookshop chain.

From Feltrinelli I might make my way to the Suhrkamp stand. The company was run by Siegfried Unseld, an arrogant man, heavy in body and heavy in mind. It was at his stand one year that I learned of the young East German writer Uwe Johnson, who was all the rage in Germany. I read *Mutmassung Uber Jacob* in German and I cannot say that I really liked it but I was most certainly impressed and decided to buy the British rights, a decision which endeared me to Unseld (to whom I am not at all sure I wished to be endeared).

This brings me to the French literary dynasty, Gallimard, who were for many years *the* great French publishing house. They certainly had many more prize winners than anyone else. Gallimard employ rights girls who invariably know their stuff. They would take me through the 'futures' list at prodigious length, a process which lasted well over an hour. Claude Gallimard himself rarely stooped to standing about at the fair. He, like other big chiefs, would hold court at his hotel.

There are two key hotels, both extremely difficult to get into: the Frankfurter Hof, in town, an old-style and superficially attractive place. The service is terrible. Breakfast, if you were foolish enough to order it in your room, could take more than an hour to arrive. The other hotel is the Hessischer Hof, near the fair. Should you be lucky enough to obtain a reservation there, unless you are a big spender, you will be allocated a tiny broom cupboard of a room looking out on to the noisy main road. This hotel has a bar called Jimmy's, considered by the literary set to be the most desirable meeting place in Frankfurt. One evening a few of us were having a drink there with Cohn-Bendit, the student rebel. The management made no comment but it just so happened that none of the reservations of those present were confirmed for the following year. That is how I lost even my broom cupboard.

Jimmy's was also the location of an amusing little Frankfurt scene. A group of publishers of various nationalities were engaged in a game, whereby each publisher was required to nominate the author they were most proud of having discovered. When it came to the turn of Tom Rosenthal he nominated Ian McEwan. This struck me, and I assume it struck everyone else present, as bizarre since it was Rosenthal who lost McEwan as an author by insisting that he produce a novel rather than publishing his superb volume of stories.

At night, a number of publishers give private dinners and occasionally the host will invite some of his authors in addition to the inevitable fellow publishers. At the Hanser party, I recall an especially jolly evening at a small table with Umberto Eco, author of *The Name of the Rose*. I imagined that as a professor of philosophy he would be rather dour. How wrong I was. A dinner of a totally different order is the buffet given by Bertelsmann, to which as many as a thousand people are invited. If you arrive early (before the jackals get at it) the sight of the food would dazzle you. It is the most spectacular-looking buffet I have ever experienced. The evening became so celebrated that Bertelsmann took to hiring special security men to ensure only those with invitations were admitted. These dinners notwithstanding, my greatest delight is derived from spending an evening *à deux* with a real friend. And my dearest in Frankfurt for some years has been Roberto Calasso, the founder of the finest publishing house to emerge in Italy in recent years. As if that were not enough, he is also an important writer and I am happy to say we are his UK publisher. In literature our tastes are similar. A contemporary writer for whom we both share the greatest passion is Bruce Chatwin.

An event of a different kind is the visit of a personality

who has been invited to the Frankfurt Book Fair to launch a book. Normally I do not bother to attend such receptions. The exception in recent years was Muhammad Ali's launch which I went to because I simply and unashamedly wanted to see the man in the flesh. I even came away with a photograph of the two of us.

Another special event that must be mentioned is the giving of the Peace Prize. This ceremony is held in the cathedral and I usually give it a miss. But one year when the recipient was the British publisher Victor Gollancz I decided to attend. I was horrified to hear Gollancz (a baptized Jew) say: 'I did not like Hitler but may his poor tormented soul rest in peace.' He spoke in German and I have translated literally and precisely, but it is of course the German words that still resonate in my mind.

I have left the 'grandest' Frankfurt social event till last. It is the lunch hosted by the Deutsche Bank, which owns several leading German publishing houses. This takes place in the penthouse on the twenty-eighth floor of the bank, and to be invited is considered an honour, granted almost exclusively to the heads of houses. Rather like being in *Who's Who*, once you are on the list you stay on the list. Guests are expected to wear a jacket and tie and they do so without exception. I confess that I used to attend simply to be there. I would have found a frankfurter or a bratwurst at one of the mobile vans outside the fair much more enjoyable. Regardless of this I continued to attend the Fischer lunch at the Deutsche Bank year after year until 1994. On that occasion, as always, I had placed a tie in my jacket pocket in readiness for the event. I walked the mile to the bank (some publishers hire a limousine) and on arrival my name was ticked off on the list of guests and I was catapulted to the twenty-eighth floor where the bar offers a choice of any drink imaginable. Half an hour later the lunch was announced and I joined the queue to the dining room. I lined up for a few minutes and then, instead of entering with the others, I slid over to the lift and asked to be taken down. I went out on to the street and walked towards the fair, leaving the bank behind. As I walked, I took off my tie and felt a sense of release. For several more years I continued to receive invitations to the lunch but of course I always declined. Eventually the invitations ceased to arrive.

MARRIAGE

REGINA AND I got married on 16 October 1987. We were woken that morning by the telephone and a voice said: 'What are you going to do?'

I asked, 'What do you mean?' and the voice replied that there had been a police announcement saying no one should travel by car and that Kent especially was out of bounds. We had slept through it, but apparently that night there had been the most horrendous storm for several decades. Regina and I wondered for a moment what we should do. But we had no alternative and so we replied, 'Let's go for it,' adding, 'But do leave as early as you possibly can.' We rang the hotel we had chosen for the wedding dinner, which was of course in Kent. Predictably there was no answer. No doubt their phone would have been knocked out.

Our formal marriage ceremony took place that morning, as planned, at Marylebone register office, although we had arranged a blessing for 6 p.m. in a church near the hotel. We set off immediately with twenty-eight pigeons that we had brought back from France stowed in the boot of the car. The journey, which would normally have taken an hour and a half at most, took six hours. On arrival we were unable to drive right up to the hotel, since it was in a park and several enormous fallen trees blocked the way.

The first guests to arrive were Roald Dahl and his wife

Liccy. Roald was not in a good mood. Being elderly and not in the best of health, he had made a reservation at a hotel some six miles from ours. On arrival, after a long journey, he rang the bell. No answer. He rang again. Still no answer. Then they stepped back and the Dahls saw that the hotel was without its roof. Clearly the owners had evacuated the place. Fortunately Roald and Liccy were able to find another hotel still functioning nearby.

The next couple to arrive at the church were Richard and Joan Branson. In a sense they were the odd couple since, not surprisingly, most of our friends were writers. I had met Richard relatively recently. I'd read a profile of him in *The Times* and thought I would really like to meet him. I rang him out of the blue, so to speak, and he invited me over that same evening, whereupon he asked me whether I would be interested in running Virgin Books. I declined, but we became fast friends and saw a good deal of each other, spending several weekends together. The Bransons came to our Welsh cottage and we stayed in their house outside Oxford.

Only half our guests made it to the church. After the blessing we went off to the hotel, where as there was no electricity at all the entire place was lit by candles. A beautiful sight. Fortunately the hotel used gas for cooking. The dinner was a triumph, the pigeons perfectly cooked, and we ended as we had begun, with champagne. By the time Regina and I went upstairs I was quite drunk and I longed to get into bed. It was not possible. Someone had made us an apple-pie bed. I later found out it was Richard Branson.

The morning after our wedding we had a very early breakfast. Having chosen Venice for our honeymoon, we decided to allow extra time lest we encountered obstacles on the way to the airport.

CARNEY

I WAS TWENTY-FOUR when I bought Carney, a remote stone cottage in the Black Mountains, on the Welsh border. My girlfriend, Martha, and I had been staying at the Llanthony Abbey Hotel, which was built in the twelfth century, and each day we went for long walks. One of these led us to the village of Capel-Y-Finn (Chapel at the End). It has only one house and a population of two. The main road leads on to Hay-on-Wye, eight miles away. At Capel-Y-Finn we turned left along an even more remote and narrow lane, passing a monastery, and then on down a hill, across a ford, and up another hill. There the road came to an end and in front of us stood a gate to the mountain. On the right a second gate led up a grass driveway. At the top of the hill five men were repairing the road which went nowhere. I asked why they were mending a road in such a remote spot. They said, 'You see that cottage [pointing up the grass driveway]? The bloke who owns it has got round the local council. We think he wants to sell his place.' So up we went. We knocked on the door and the couple who lived there asked us in for a cup of tea. I mentioned what the road men had said: 'Yes, it is so,' the man replied. He explained that he and his wife had lived in the cottage for thirty years but now that they were in their eighties, they found the winters on the mountain too rough. Their daughter lived in Portsmouth and they had decided to look for a house near her.

I asked the price they wanted and they named a figure. To my astonishment I found myself saying that I would like to buy the cottage, even though I had only seen a single room, the one in which we had tea. I proposed that they let me know when they had found something in Portsmouth and then we left.

A few months later the couple wrote asking whether I had been serious. 'Yes, of course,' I replied, and sent them the name and address of my solicitor. The cottage was a magical place, poised on the mountain with sheep and wild ponies scattered upon the hillside. After the contracts had been exchanged I was so excited I could not sleep for weeks and then, on completion, when the house was mine, I drove down to look at it properly for the first time. I wanted to share this experience with a person for whom I care deeply. It was Doris Lessing with whom I went.

I did not know when I bought Carney that there were two nearby literary connections. One was Eric Gill, the designer and sculptor, who wrote his autobiography at the monastery on to which the cottage looks. The other was Francis Kilvert, the Victorian pastor from Clyro, just outside Hay. His diaries are a classic of English literature and in them he writes of the countryside around my cottage. Both books, by coincidence, were published by Jonathan Cape, many years before I was there of course. Later, the cottage has inspired a number of other writers, including, as I have already mentioned, Bruce Chatwin, who spent five months living in Carney, writing *On the Black Hill*. Another was Allen Ginsberg, who wrote his poem 'Wales Visitation' whilst staying at Carney with me.

Nearby Hay-on-Wye is known for its annual literary festival. It was there, one year, that I had a poignant encounter with Eddie Portman, who was President of the Festival and gave the opening address. We had last seen each other forty years previously when Eddie's father, who thought it a good plan for him to work in a publishing house, had arranged for Eddie to come to MacGibbon & Kee, at the same time as I was there. I cannot say that Eddie did much work. When he inherited the title, becoming Lord Portman, with vast estates in London, he also inherited thousands of head of cattle and came to live near Hay.

Over the years at the Festival I have met hundreds of writers in encounters that take place spontaneously and casually, in the lecture tents, on the lawn and in the pub. And then occasionally there would be a special and private event. One such was a dinner in honour of William Golding, whom I had met several times previously although I had never spent an entire evening in his company. The night of the dinner in Hay he was in particularly good form, relaxed, jovial and happy. It is not possible to define precisely what made it so but the dinner was an exceptional one for all of us. Regina and I happened to be sitting near Golding and his wife and they invited us to stay with them for a weekend in Dorset. We were flattered and happy to accept. Alas, before we could do so he had died.

I will mention two other dinners. On both occasions Peter Florence, who runs the Festival (and who had invited me to become a Vice-President), had asked if I could help out, since he was engaged elsewhere and wanted me to host dinner on his behalf. The first was a disaster. Our guest was the brilliant critic George Steiner and I chose to take him to the Walnut Tree, by far the best restaurant in the region and (according to *The Good Food Guide*) just about the best country restaurant in England. It happens to be some twenty miles from Hay, but I knew George rather well and thought he would find it worth the drive. I led the way; he followed. After five or six miles he honked and we stopped. He demanded to know how much further it was. Five miles on and he honked again. The same question. Then a third time, before we finally arrived at the restaurant. When we were seated George calmed down and we were able to enjoy our meal. We even had some conversation. The moment I had paid the bill he got up and left. By the time I reached the door he was in his car. He revved up and was gone. Subsequently I received an extraordinary letter from him. He said that my behaviour pointed to 'mental derangement' and went on to state that if anything had gone amiss 'on that difficult drive back' he would have contacted the police.

The second occasion was an entirely happy one. Peter asked me if I could possibly take Wilfred Thesiger out to dinner. What a question! Thesiger was the last of the great travel writers and his accounts of his journeys through Arab lands are without parallel. He was then in his eighties and lived in Africa. Thesiger is a myth. I had never met him. It had not occurred to me that I ever would. And now, here we were in a modest pub outside Hay, having dinner together. He was a little hard of hearing and so am I. But somehow we managed to communicate.

POETS

Whilst I greatly enjoy publishing poetry, I am far less confident of my judgement of it than that of prose and especially fiction. Nevertheless I have published a good number of poets, many of them important. They include five Nobel Prize winners: Seferis, Cavafy, Nellie Sachs, Pablo Neruda and Derek Walcott. The last of these is the only one for whom I really feel I can take any credit in that I published him from the very beginning when he was unknown. Derek is Trinidadian and a number of his early poems appeared in the *London Magazine*. It was the editor, Alan Ross, who drew his work to my attention. I responded to his poetry right away and we put together a first collection of lyrical and vibrant poems called *In a Green Night*. With some confidence I sent a proof copy to the highly literary publishing house of Farrar, Straus in New York. To my enormous delight they bought the American rights, a most unusual event for an unknown poet. We and Farrar, Straus published several further books by Derek, and then Roger Straus took it upon himself to suggest that Derek leave Cape and go to a more important British publisher of poetry, namely Faber and Faber. I cannot say it was a gracious act on Roger's part given the fact that he 'owed' Walcott entirely to me, but as Kurt Vonnegut would say, 'So it goes.' By the time Derek won the Nobel Prize in 1992 I was no longer his publisher. Of course this did not diminish my sense of pride but it did affect my travel plans.

The other monumentally important poet whom we published and introduced to an English-speaking audience was Pablo Neruda. He had long been acknowledged as a great poet in Chile and it is strange that he should have been neglected in England for so many years. We published his *Twenty Love Poems*, his *Macchu Picchu* and a very large volume of selected poems. He came over to see us several times. This bulk of a man with a most benign smile and a face like a turtle became a familiar sight at Bedford Square. He loved to eat and of the restaurants to which I took him the Connaught was his favourite.

Great poets apart, I have also brought to the Cape list a few 'light' poets, including Roger McGough, Adrian Mitchell, Adrian Henri and Leonard Cohen. Each of them has had a measure of success, and one of them sold hundreds of thousands of copies. That was of course Leonard Cohen.

ALLEN GINSBERG

I FIRST MET Allen Ginsberg in Cuba. He was already extremely famous, especially for *Howl*, *Kaddish* and many other little black Ferlingetti volumes of poetry. Allen was part of a delegation of writers invited by the Cuban government, and I (who had not been invited) somehow attached myself to the group. Other members included the Mexican essayist and poet Octavio Paz, who subsequently won the Nobel Prize. We spent some days in Havana where we visited Ernest Hemingway's home and were shown the desk at which Hemingway wrote, always standing up, and the tower he built for himself to write better, and in which he never wrote a word. Then we toured the country in a minibus. Allen and I liked each other immediately and we became inseparable.

Just outside Havana there was a war memorial which encompassed an American airplane the Cubans had shot down. Allen spontaneously and irreverently jumped on to the plane and flung his arms in the air in a gesture of victory. A photograph I took of him astride the plane has been reprinted around the world. One place where it was reproduced particularly effectively was in the *Paris Review* alongside a lengthy interview with Allen.

On our journey around the country, a delegate died of a heart attack. One minute he was sitting with us in the bus and the next, we heard he was dead. The body was laid out for viewing and the delegates trooped reverently past it. I declined. To do so would have been too ghoulish, after seeing the man alive just half an hour previously. Allen said, 'Tom, don't be silly, just think of it as a sack of potatoes.' His words have always stuck in my mind.

Back in Havana after six days we were taken to hear Castro give one of his enormously lengthy speeches. It lasted several hours. He spoke in Spanish but I managed to understand some of what he said, including a tirade against homosexuals. That night the police took it upon themselves to round up hundreds of men and put them in gaol. Allen was one of the leaders of the protest that took place the following day. Later, the police arrived at his hotel room, and I stood by as he bundled up his belongings. Allen-style, he travelled light. The police escorted him to the airport whence he was to be extradited. I was allowed to accompany him to the departure lounge. Before leaving, Allen, in his typical orderly and caring fashion, gave me several farewell notes to distribute. We hugged each other and expressed the hope that we would soon meet again.

A few months after Allen's premature departure from Havana, he wrote to me from New York, saying he had been invited to do some readings in England and asking whether he could stay with me. Of course he could. I had a whole house to myself in Chalcot Crescent but I must confess I was a little nervous. His reputation was that of a somewhat wild person and I valued the calm of my home. As it turned out, Allen was meticulous and ever thoughtful. If we were planning to have dinner together at home, just the two of us, at say 8 p.m., he would telephone when he thought he might be even twenty minutes late. Whilst I had expected Allen to stay a week or two, in fact he stayed for two months, but he was always a pleasure to be with. Another surprise was that every now and then he would ask me for some money. This was not regarded as a loan and the amount was unspecified. I would give him £10 or so and he would take it without a word. I never questioned this but it seemed strange since Allen was extremely highly paid for his readings. In addition I imagine he earned a great deal from the sale of his books.

While Allen was in London I introduced him to Barry Hall, who ran Cape Goliard, a company we had recently formed. This represented, to quote the poet Nathaniel Tarn, whose brainchild it was, 'a little press within a large house'. All the books were printed by Barry on a hand-operated letter-press machine and most of them were heavily illustrated by contemporary artists. They were produced on high-quality paper and in small editions, usually of between 250 and 500 copies. The idea appealed to Allen and he gave us a manuscript for publication called *TV Baby Poems*.

On Allen's subsequent trip to England I took him to Carney in the Black Mountains. He fell in love with the place, as I knew he would. At dinner on our first evening Allen brought out a small screwtop tin and showed me the contents – two small white pills wrapped in cotton wool. He said, 'These are LSD. I thought you might like to try it. If you don't want to, I won't either. But you need not be nervous. If you take the pill I will wait to make sure you are OK before I follow you.' His degree of caring was seductive. I had never taken LSD but had often thought of doing so, and this seemed like the ideal opportunity, with the perfect person and in the perfect place, in beautiful surroundings and far away from noise of any kind. Allen suggested we wait until the following morning so that the effect would have worn off by the evening, otherwise, he said, the pills would keep us awake all night. I know that LSD can have a very bad effect on some people, but I had a hunch I would be all right and that is how it turned out. I took the pill and looked out of my sitting-room window on to the mountainside opposite. The mountain gradually turned a reddish-brown and the earth began to run down the hillside like lava.

Some three or four hours after we had taken the pills, Allen proposed we go for a walk up the mountain. I was a little fearful in case I was unable to make the climb. 'There is nothing to fear,' said Allen, and he led the way up. There he taught me a mantra. I have continued to use it for forty years. It goes UM, UM SA RA WAH, BUDDHA, DA KEEN E EYE, BEN ZA, WAN NIYE, BEN ZA, BE RO, ZA NI YE UM, UM UM, PEY PEY PEY SO HA. I use it at home, in the bath, on walks, and best of all, on ski lifts.

The hills surrounding my cottage are dotted with sheep and Allen saw us as just two more sheep below the sky. He was immensely moved by the landscape and in the afternoon, still heavily under the influence of the drug, he began to write a poem called 'Wales Visitation'. On the way back to London I had a sense of driving over the earth, the earth that was underneath the tarmac of the road. This sensation stayed with me for a number of years. Even now it returns from time to time.

Some years later I visited Allen at his home in Greenwich Village. I was curious to see the apartment behind the address from which I had received so many letters, the home to which he returned between journeys but rarely stayed for long. The place was a dreadful mess: piles of clothing flung all over the floor, piles of washing-up in the sink. Clearly Allen's friend and lover, Peter Orlovski, was not interested in order. It pained me that such a special human being as Allen could be so careless about the surroundings in which he lived.

Allen was the most spontaneous, the most unpretentious, the warmest, the most adorable, the most humble human being I have ever met. When I read of his death, I felt a profound sadness. I loved you, Allen.

POSTSCRIPT

I HAVE ATTEMPTED to convey the excitement of publishing these authors. Frequently they came into my life by chance. I have often been asked to define what makes one decide on a particular book. This is a difficult question to answer. The choice is so personal, so subjective. There are no rules. I can say that for me the selection of a book and an author is rarely for commercial reasons. To publish well the publisher must be passionate about the book for its own sake. For me to be so I must truly care about the book and for me to care I must admire it for its quality. That is my only rule. Once the choice is made the task begins. It is to transmit one's conviction first within the publishing house and then to the outside world.

I would like to explain how this book came about. From time to time in recent years I was approached by various publishers with the suggestion that I should write a memoir. Such an approach was of course always flattering and especially when it came from someone like Lord Weidenfeld. He and I invariably met at the Frankfurt Book Fair. Then one year George was especially effusive and suggested that I come to lunch at his grand Chelsea flat overlooking the Thames. The day after my return from Frankfurt his secretary rang to propose a date. I must confess that whilst I was exceedingly doubtful about this project I could not resist accepting the invitation. I was eager to see George's legendary persuasive powers in action. On the day of the lunch I arrived convinced that I did not want to write the book and I left convinced that I could and should write it. Shortly afterwards I was invited to one of George's famous parties. John Gross, the editor of the *Times Literary Supplement*, was talking to Harold Wilson and Antonia Fraser when he turned to me and said simply, 'Congratulations.' I had no idea what he was talking about and so I asked what the congratulations were in aid of. He told me that the party was for me and my book! A week later a contract arrived. I have never signed it but I kept the document as a souvenir. The extraordinary thing is that neither George nor anyone from his office ever mentioned either the book or the contract again.

Some years later a young man as persuasive as George called Peter Straus approached me. It was at our third or possibly fourth lunch together that I agreed. Not long afterwards Peter left the publishing house of Picador to become a literary agent. He was succeeded by Andrew Kidd and it is my very good fortune that Andrew has taken the greatest possible interest in the book, even to the extent of abandoning his family to come out to France for a weekend. And then at Picador I am equally fortunate to have Sam Humphreys as my editor. Her taste is immaculate and her patience infinite. In short, she is the perfect editor.

I wish to thank Liccy Dahl for her permission to use Roald's letter and Doris Lessing and Kurt Vonnegut for permission to use their letters.

And finally I would like especially to thank Quentin Blake. There are many demands upon his time and yet when I asked whether he would consider producing some drawings for this book he agreed without hesitation. For me, Quentin is the perfect artist in that his drawings capture the essence of things. In addition he is a joy to work with.

I now spend more time in my house in France than I do in

London. I am frequently asked whether I have retired. There are many who dream of retirement. I am not one of them. And so I answer that I now work part-time. I arrived at Jonathan Cape in my twenties, forty years ago. I have never considered an alternative and I have never considered giving up. I find my publishing life so exhilarating that I cannot imagine the adventure coming to an end. Though of course I know that one day it must.

INDEX